GRAINS AS MAINS

Jodi Moreno
Sarah W. Caron

LONDON, NEW YORK, MELBOURNE, MUNICH, AND DELHI

US Editor and Consultant Rebecca Warren
US Associate Managing Editor Allison Singer
Senior Editor Vanessa Daubney
Senior Art Editor Sara Robin
Managing Editor Dawn Henderson
Managing Art Editor Christine Keilty
Jacket Art Editor Kathryn Wilding
Pre-Production Producer Rebecca Fallowfield
Senior Producer Jen Scothern
Art Director Peter Luff
Publisher Peggy Vance

DK INDIA
Editor Neha Ruth Samuel
Senior Art Editor Ira Sharma
Art Editor Neha Wahi
Assistant Art Editor Pallavi Kapur
Managing Editor Alicia Ingty
Managing Art Editor Navidita Thapa
Pre-Production Manager Sunil Sharma
DTP Designers Rajdeep Singh, Manish Upreti, Satish Chandra Gaur

First American edition, 2015
Published in the United States by DK Publishing,
345 Hudson Street, New York, NY 10014

15 16 17 18 19   10 9 8 7 6 5 4 3 2 1
001–271731–Mar/2015

A catalog record for this book is available
from the Library of Congress.
ISBN 978-1-4654-3180-6

Color reproduction by Altaimage LTD
Printed and bound in Hung Hing

DK books are available at special discounts when purchased in
bulk for sales promotions, premiums, fund-raising, or educational
use. For details, contact: DK Publishing Special Markets, 345
Hudson Street, New York, NY 10014 or Special Sales@dk.com.

www.dk.com

CONTENTS

FOREWORD

Until a few years ago, when (or *if*) we thought about grains, the only ones that came to mind were probably wheat, barley, cornmeal, and maybe farro. Then quinoa came along and changed everything.

I remember seeing more and more recipes including this mysterious grain. What is quinoa, I wondered, mispronouncing it as *kin-oh-a*? I learned that it's actually pronounced *keen-wah* and it's a delicious, nutritional powerhouse that can be used in numerous ways. After cooking my first batch, I was hooked, and immediately wanted to try other ancient grains. Millet and amaranth made their way into my repertoire and, since then, a dozen more have won a spot in my pantry.

When eaten in their whole form, these ancient grains are some of the best foods you can eat. It is recommended that we consume at least three servings of whole grains daily, and the list of health benefits of a diet that incorporates them is long. The ancient grains selected for inclusion in this book are the most well known and versatile. Not only are they good for us, but they also add a whole new level of variety to our cooking. As the recipes in *Grains as Mains* show, these grains are no longer being used just as a side dish; they can be enjoyed for breakfast, lunch, dinner, and dessert, and can often be found as the main ingredient (or protein) in a dish.

Whether ancient grains are new to you, or even if you have been eating them for a long time, I hope that the information and recipes in this book will encourage you to include grains more often in your cooking and that these dishes will give you as much pleasure as we have had in creating them.

JODI MORENO

WHAT ARE GRAINS?

iN WiTH THE OLD

WHAT ARE ANCIENT GRAiNS?

The term "ancient grains" describes a number of grains or seeds that are enjoying a resurgence in popularity, but which in fact have been grown and eaten for hundreds of thousands of years by different cultures around the world.

A few of these grains, such as cornmeal (polenta) and wheat, are used readily in modern cooking. However, for others, it is only a matter of time until these grains become household names. As you will see from the recipes in this book, grains are much more than just a side dish. You can incorporate them into every meal—from breakfast to dinner, and (of course) dessert.

EAT LiKE AN EGYPTiAN

The history of ancient grains goes back thousands of years, when ancient civilizations relied on these grains as a source of energy and protein. Some grains, such as farro, are known to date back to the Egyptian era, when it was used in bread making.

Nowadays, grains are produced and harvested all across the world, and many can still be found in the areas from which they originated. Amaranth and quinoa originated, and are mostly grown, in South American regions; kamut and farro originated in Egypt; teff and barley are from Ethopia; and millet is mainly from Africa and Asia.

Unlike many crops, these "newer" ancient grains are very much unchanged and free of hybridization (genetic modification), which is something most people are trying to avoid.

CARBOHYDRATE KiNGS AND QUEENS

Whole grains are by far the best source of energy from a carbohydrate food. With many also high in fiber and protein (quinoa and amaranth are complete proteins, meaning that they are great alternatives to meat), these grains deliver the consistent energy we need, but they also come with a variety of nutrients and health benefits. Grains are low-fat, complex carbohydrates, making you feel satisfied for longer, and they can help to maintain a healthy weight by curbing cravings and the desire to overeat.

Each grain contains many essential vitamins, nutrients, and antioxidants (for more information, see pages 18–19). Plus, whole grains include disease-fighting phytonutrients (plant-based minerals that provide essential antioxidants), which are such a crucial part of a healthy diet.

Research is showing that, when enjoyed regularly, these grains can help control blood sugar and cholesterol levels and contribute toward reducing the likelihood of problems with high blood pressure, or strokes, heart disease, diabetes, and cancer.

QUALITY AND QUANTITY

Always buy your grains from a reliable source and, if purchasing them from a supermarket or health food store, check the label. If you are using a whole grain, you want to make sure the whole grain, including the bran, is intact and that it has not been processed, which would remove a lot of the essential nutrients.

HEALTH AWARENESS

Many ancient grains are gluten-free and are completely safe for people who are gluten intolerant. If someone has mild gluten intolerance, they may also be able to eat some of the other grains, such as spelt, but for those with a more severe gluten intolerance, such as celiac sufferers, only choose grains that are said to be from a dedicated gluten-free facility.

GRAINS FOR LITTLE PEOPLE

Grains are safe to eat for children over the age of 12 months. Government guidelines will vary, but most recommend that you do not feed children under the age of five only whole grains because they need to get nutrients from a wide variety of foods. When feeding grains to young children, it is best to soak the grains overnight. This will allow children to digest the grains and absorb the nutrients more easily.

THE GRAIN STORE
GLUTEN-FREE GRAINS

Whole grains contain all edible parts of the grain and are packed with nutrients including protein, fiber, B vitamins, antioxidants, and minerals. For anyone suffering from gluten intolerance, the following grains can play a huge part in a healthy, balanced diet.

QUINOA

Quinoa is a small round grain that has a slightly bitter flavor and a firm texture when cooked. Discovered by the Incas, Quinoa was first grown thousands of years ago, and today the most widely cultivated varieties are white, red, and black. Due to its high oil content, Quinoa is best stored in an airtight container in the fridge.

BUCKWHEAT

Originating from Asia, buckwheat is a fruit seed related to rhubarb and sorrel and has a unique triangular shape. Buckwheat is one of the healthiest, nuttiest, and most versatile whole grains. It is available unroasted or roasted. Stored correctly in a sealed container in a cool, dry place, whole buckwheat can last up to 12 months.

TEFF

Teff is a tiny grain, similar in size to a poppy seed, and is available in a variety of colors, including white, red, and dark brown. Found predominantly in Ethiopia and Eritrea, teff can thrive in difficult climates, including waterlogged soils and during droughts. Stored in tightly sealed plastic or glass containers, teff will keep for up to 12 months.

MiLLET

Millet is the name given to a group of small round grains, and the hulled variety is most commonly available. It was widely used in Asia before rice became the staple grain in the region. Millet becomes rancid fairly quickly, but if kept in a sealed container, it will remain fresh for two months if stored in a cupboard, or for four months in the fridge.

CORNMEAL

Cornmeal, also often referred to as polenta, is believed to have been discovered by Native Americans circa 5000 BC and is derived from ground, dried corn. Its consistency can be fine, medium, or coarse. Cornmeal can retain its freshness for up to 12 months when sealed and stored in a cool, dry place.

SORGHUM

Native to Africa, Sorghum is a small, round grain, ranging in color from white and brown to red and black. White sorghum is most commonly used and can be ground and substituted for wheat flour. Left whole, it makes fantastic popcorn. Stored in a container in a cool, dark place, it will keep for at least 12 months.

AMARANTH

Amaranth is a tiny seed with a nutty flavor that was discovered more than 8,000 years ago by the ancient Aztecs, who relied on it as one of their staple foods. Amaranth will lose its flavor and become bitter if it is stored in a warm location, but it will keep well for up to 12 months in a cool, dry pantry.

GRAINS CONTAINING GLUTEN

For anyone who is sensitive to gluten, a protein found in wheat and other grains, such as barley, it is best to avoid the grains shown here. In general, when buying grains, make sure they are tightly sealed. If you notice a musty or oily aroma, then the grains are not in the best condition.

BULGUR WHEAT

Bulgur wheat is parboiled, dried, then cracked, and is pale brown in color with an irregular shape. When cooked, it has a delicious nutty flavor and a chewy texture. It is popular in Middle Eastern and Mediterranean cuisines. This grain should be stored in an airtight container and keeps well in a cool, dry place for up to a year.

BARLEY

A fabulously versatile grain, barley has a long and interesting history originating in Ethiopia and South East Asia over 10,000 years ago. The most common form is pearl barley, which has the outer husk and bran layers removed. Barley can have a shelf life of up to one year if stored in an airtight container in a cool place.

KAMUT

Kamut is a trademark name for a type of khorasan grain, believed to have derived from ancient Egypt. It is a brown grain with a long shape, similar to basmati rice, that has a nutty flavor and a chewy texture when cooked. If stored in an airtight container away from heat and moisture, kamut may keep for over 12 months.

FREEKEH

Freekeh is an ancient Middle Eastern grain and is actually wheat that is harvested early, while the grains are still green. The kernels are roasted, dried, and rubbed, resulting in a slightly smoky flavor and nutty texture. The grain should be stored in a sealed jar and will retain its flavor and freshness for up to a year.

FARRO

Farro is the Italian name for emmer wheat, a hard wheat from western Asia. Similar in texture to pearl barley, farro is popular in Italy for its distinctive nutty roasted flavor and chewy texture. It is versatile and can be added to soups, risottos, and salads. Farro will keep for up to one year if stored in a sealed container in a cool, dark place.

WHEAT BERRIES

Wheat berries are not berries, but the whole kernels from a wheat plant with the husks removed, and are available as a hard or soft grain. They have a delicate, creamy, nutty flavor and are a light, reddish brown color. Wheat berries can be ground into flour or used whole and should be stored in a cool, dry place.

SPELT

Originating in Iran and parts of southern Europe, spelt is a relative of wheat and is one of the oldest grains. It has an oval-like shape and a characteristic nutty flavor. This grain can be used whole or can be ground into flour. Stored in a cool, dry place and sealed tightly, spelt will remain fresh for at least 12 months.

PERFECTLY COOKED

To ensure perfect results when cooking grains, follow the steps on pages 20 and 22–23. Rinse grains as necessary and use a **heavy-bottomed saucepan** with a lid to cook them in. Use the guides below to make sure that your grains are perfectly cooked.

◄ COOKED AMARANTH
Amaranth should be cooked one part grain to three parts boiling water, then simmered gently for about 25 minutes. Cooked amaranth is rather sticky, but remains crunchy on the outside and soft inside.

COOKED FREEKEH ▲
Freekeh is extremely easy to cook. The cooking times and liquid ratios vary depending on whether you are using whole grain or cracked freekeh, so follow the directions on the package.

COOKED BUCKWHEAT ►
Buckwheat should be rinsed thoroughly before cooking. Add one part buckwheat to two parts boiling water or stock and cook for about 12–15 minutes. It also cooks well by absorption or steaming methods.

◄ COOKED FARRO
Farro is available in different varieties, and the whole-grain kind takes longer to cook than semi-pearled or pearled. The easiest way to cook it is in boiling water (in a 1:2 ratio of grain to water) for approximately 15–20 minutes. Its chewy texture makes farro a fantastic substitute for rice and pasta.

COOKED KAMUT ▲
Presoaking kamut is optional but will significantly speed up the cooking process. Bring the measured water to a boil (use a 1:2 ratio of grain to water), add the drained, soaked grain, then cover, and simmer for 30–40 minutes. **Spelt** can be cooked in a similar way.

COOKED QUINOA ▶

Rinse quinoa before cooking to remove the bitter coating. Boil for 10–15 minutes. The cooked grains quadruple in size and become translucent. **Millet** can be cooked similarly, but does not need rinsing.

◀ COOKED SORGHUM

Rinse sorghum before cooking, then cook in a ratio of one part grain to three parts water or stock. Bring to a boil in a pan with a tight fitting lid, then simmer for up to an hour until tender.

COOKED TEFF ▶

Cooking teff depends on how it is being served. It can be cooked in boiling water or sprinkled in soups, salads, or baked goods, adding flavor and texture. It is also eaten as a cereal.

◀ COOKED WHEAT BERRIES

Cook wheat berries in a 1:2 ratio of grain to water. Add the grains to boiling water in a pan, cover, and simmer for about 60 minutes until the grains are soft. Soaking wheat berries overnight can help to reduce the cooking time.

FLOUR AND FLAKES

These flours and flakes contain the whole grain. Stored carefully and covered, they will keep for 3 months in a cool, dry place out of direct sunlight. Gluten-free flours produce crumblier baked goods, so it helps to add extra liquid.

AMARANTH FLOUR Amaranth flour is perfect for gluten-free cooking and baking, and can be used in cake, cookie, bread, and pastry recipes.

BUCKWHEAT FLOUR Gluten free and ideal for making pancakes, scones, and cookies, this flour can be added to other flours for bread making.

KAMUT FLOUR This wheat flour has a smooth, buttery, and nutty flavor. It can be substituted in any recipe using regular wheat flour.

MILLET FLAKES Wheat and gluten free, they are often used in muesli or hot cereals, or in crumbles and cookies for added texture.

QUINOA FLAKES Made by flattening unprocessed, raw quinoa seeds, these are high in protein, gluten free and can be used for muesli or a hot cereal.

TEFF FLOUR A 100 percent whole flour, it is creamy brown in color with a unique sweet and malty flavor and is ideal for baking.

GRAIN POWER

Grains are an excellent source of protein, carbohydrates, fiber, and many minerals and vitamins. The information in this section shows how a portion of each grain (1½oz/45g of the dry grain) can contribute to the recommended daily intakes of these vital nutrients. The table below explains what the functions of each nutrient are in maintaining a healthy body.

KNOW YOUR NUTRIENTS

NUTRIENTS	GOOD FOR
Protein	general health and growth
Carbohydrates	providing energy
Calcium	bones and teeth; regulating muscle contractions
Fiber	digestion; preventing heart disease and diabetes
Iron	making red blood cells
Magnesium	muscle and nerve function; controlling glucose levels; regulating blood pressure
Phosphorus	bones and teeth; maintaining vital organs
Potassium	regulating blood pressure; keeping kidneys healthy
Sodium	muscles and nerves
Zinc	growth and development; taste and smell
Copper	maintaining vital organs; metabolism
Manganese	bones; producing collagen
Selenium	reproduction; metabolism; protecting against infection

VITAMINS	GOOD FOR
Thiamin (B1)	metabolism; processing energy
Riboflavin (B2)	building blood cells; metabolism
Niacin (B3)	processing energy; protecting against free radicals; metabolism
Pantothenic (B5)	processing energy; building hormones; immune system
Pyridoxine (B6)	proper growth; organ development; healthy blood; good cholesterol levels
Folic Acid (B9)	blood cells; regulating the nervous system (essential during pregnancy)
Vitamin C	blood cells; healing wounds

THE GOODIES IN GRAINS

The calorific content and amounts of protein, carbohydrates, fiber, and significant levels of minerals and vitamins are listed here per portion (45g/1½oz dry weight) of each grain featured in the book. The grains also contain traces of other nutrients.

CORNMEAL

Calories 163 **Protein** 3.65g
Carbohydrates 34.60g **Fiber** 3.3g

Good source of magnesium; phosphorus; manganese; selenium; Vitamins B2 and B3

QUINOA

Calories 166 **Protein** 6.35g
Carbohydrates 28.87g **Fiber** 3.2g

Good source of iron; copper; Vitamins B1 and B6

Excellent source of magnesium; phosphorus; manganese; folate

AMARANTH

Calories 167 **Protein** 6.10g
Carbohydrates 29.36g **Fiber** 3.0g

Good source of iron; copper; selenium; Vitamin B6

Excellent source of magnesium; phosphorus

Provides 50% of RDI of manganese

FARRO

Calories 162 **Protein** 5.74g
Carbohydrates 32.55g **Fiber** 4.4g

Good source of magnesium; zinc

Excellent source of Vitamin B3

SORGHUM

Calories 166 **Protein** 6.35g
Carbohydrates 28.87g **Fiber** 3.2g

Good source of phosphorus; Vitamin B6

Excellent source of magnesium

BARLEY

Calories 159 **Protein** 5.62g
Carbohydrates 33.7g **Fiber** 7.8g

Good source of magnesium; phosphorus; copper; Vitamin B3

Excellent source of manganese; selenium; Vitamin B1

FREEKEH

Calories 160 **Protein** 6.42g
Carbohydrates 32.14g **Fiber** 6.4g

Good source of calcium; magnesium; potassium; zinc; Vitamins B1 and B2

Excellent source of iron; copper

SPELT

Calories 166 **Protein** 6.35g
Carbohydrates 28.87g **Fiber** 3.2g

Good source of iron; magnesium; phosphorus; copper; manganese; Vitamins B1 and B3

Provides 50% of RDI of manganese

BUCKWHEAT

Calories 154 **Protein** 5.96g
Carbohydrates 32.18g **Fiber** 4.5g

Good source of phosphorus; Vitamins B2 and B3

Excellent source of magnesium; copper; manganese

KAMUT

Calories 152 **Protein** 6.54g
Carbohydrates 31.76g **Fiber** 5.0g

Good source of phosphorus; potassium; zinc; Vitamin B3

Excellent source of Vitamin B1

Provides 50% of RDI of manganese; selenium

TEFF

Calories 165 **Protein** 5.98g
Carbohydrates 31.59g **Fiber** 3.6g

Good source of iron; phosphorus; zinc; Vitamins B1 and B6

Excellent source of magnesium; copper

Provides 50% of RDI of Vitamin C and 100% of RDI of manganese

BULGUR WHEAT

Calories 154 **Protein** 5.53g
Carbohydrates 34.14g **Fiber** 8.2g

Good source of magnesium; phosphorus; Vitamin B3

Provides 50% of RDI of manganese

MILLET

Calories 170 **Protein** 4.96g
Carbohydrates 32.78g **Fiber** 3.8g

Good source of magnesium; phosphorus; copper; Vitamins B1 and B3

Excellent source of manganese

WHEAT BERRIES

Calories 163 **Protein** 6.70g
Carbohydrates 32.55g **Fiber** 5.74g

Good source of iron (white); magnesium; phosphorus; Vitamins B1 and B3

Excellent source of selenium

Provides 50% of RDI of manganese (red)

Good source = circa 10% of the recommended daily intake · Excellent source = circa 20% of the recommended daily intake

BE PREPARED

Grains are easy to prepare, but each grain has a slightly different preparation method. The recipe will mention any extra steps needed to prepare the grain; some will take a few more steps than others. When reading a recipe, note which ones need extra time to rinse, soak, toast, pop, or cook the grain.

RiNSE

Most grains do not need rinsing, except quinoa, but it is beneficial. Run the grain under cold water in a fine mesh sieve immediately before cooking.

SOAK

Soak grains that take longer to cook. Place the grain in a bowl, cover with cold water, and leave it overnight. Drain and rinse before cooking.

POP

Heat a pan over medium-high heat. Add a small amount of the grain. As it heats up, the grain will start to pop. Watch it carefully, so it doesn't burn.

ROAST

Roasting adds a nutty or crunchy taste. Spread the grain on a baking sheet and bake for about 5 minutes, or according the recipe's instructions.

TOAST

Toasting can enhance a grain's flavor.
Heat a pan over medium-high heat and
add the grain. Shake the pan gently
so that the grain turns
an even color.

COOK THE PERFECT GRAiN

There are a variety of cooking methods you can choose from to cook your grain. it all depends on what equipment you own and what works best for you, but you can always rely on boiling any grain if you do not own a rice steamer or pressure cooker.

BOiL

1 For information on cooking times and liquid-to-grain ratio, see pages 16–17. To cook all grains, you can either bring the grain and liquid to a boil or add the grain to boiling water.

2 Reduce the heat, and simmer until the grain is fully cooked. Some grains will absorb the water, and others will need to be drained after cooking.

USING A RICE STEAMER

An easy way to cook grains, the benefit of a rice steamer is that once you have added the liquid and grain, you can leave it to do its work. Instructions and timings for using individual steamers will vary, but the results are good.

USING A PRESSURE COOKER

This is ideal for cooking wheat berries, barley, spelt, and kamut, which all have longer cooking times. But all grains should cook in about half the time. Treat the grain as you would rice, but adjust the timing according to the grain.

STICKY MATTERS—A COUPLE OF HANDY TIPS

It takes a little while to get accustomed to cooking different grains and, as with rice and pasta, you may run into some common problems.

If your grains get stuck to the bottom of the saucepan, add a very small amount of water while the heat is on low and use a wooden spoon to loosen the grains. Do this until the water has been absorbed.

To soak up extra moisture, turn the heat off, drape a dish towel over the pan, and place the lid on top. Let it sit for another 5–10 minutes.

GRAiN TEASERS

Cooking with grains is simple and in most cases boiling them is enough, but some recipes call for different techniques, so the following instructions will explain some procedures in more detail and, hopefully, allow you to devise your own dishes.

MAKiNG GRANOLA

1 To prepare the granola, preheat the oven to 300°F (150°C), then mix the dry ingredients together in a large bowl. Pour in the wet mixture of honey (or maple syrup), oil and any additional ingredient, and mix well with a spoon until combined.

2 Place the granola mixture on a baking sheet and spread evenly. Bake for 30 minutes until crispy, then transfer to a plate and leave to cool.

MAKING POLENTA

1 Pour the measured water into a pan and bring to a boil, reduce the heat, then gradually add the weighed polenta, stirring continuously. Stir for a minute or two until it starts to thicken.

2 Reduce the heat and continue stirring until the polenta begins to come away from the sides of the pan. Polenta can take 45 minutes to cook, while instant varieties can be ready in about 5 minutes.

3 To use as slices, transfer the polenta to a greased baking sheet, and spread it with a spatula until it is level. Allow the polenta to stand for 30 minutes to cool and firm up, then cut into slicess.

4 Once the polenta has been cut into slices, heat some oil and butter in a griddle pan over medium heat and fry the polenta for 2–3 minutes on each side, until golden.

MAKING RISOTTO

1 To prepare risotto, heat butter and oil in a large nonstick pan and gently cook the onion and any additional vegetables until soft. Add the grain, stirring continuously, until shiny and transparent.

2 Add white wine, if using, and simmer over gentle heat until evaporated. Pour in the hot stock, a ladleful at a time, stirring the mixture with each addition until the stock is fully absorbed.

3 Reduce the heat and simmer the risotto for 30 minutes, stirring occasionally, adding liquid when required until the grain is cooked, but still firm. The risotto should be creamy and slightly wet.

4 Finally, stir in any remaining ingredients such as grated Parmesan, butter, or fresh herbs. Allow the risotto to stand for 3–4 minutes, so that the flavors develop and the liquid is absorbed.

MAKING PATTIES

1 To prepare patties, place all the ingredients in a mixing bowl and bring the mixture together using a fork. Divide the mixture into equal portions and carefully roll into balls.

2 Using slightly wet hands, flatten the balls into rounds about ½–¾in (1.5–2cm) thick. Transfer the patties to a plate, cover with plastic wrap, and leave in the fridge to firm up.

DRINKS AND SMOOTHIES

Add liquid to a blender, such as cow, soy, or almond milk, yogurt, or fruit juice. Then add your choice of fruit, vegetables, and cooked grains and blitz for 1 minute until smooth.

BATCH COOKING AND FREEZING

Batch cooking and freezing grain dishes is a great way to avoid waste and save money. You can freeze most dishes, but always cool them completely before freezing. Place them in a suitable container, leaving some space for expansion, and seal tightly to prevent freezer burn. Label with a date and description.

BREAKFAST AND BRUNCH

WHEAT BERRY MUESLI POTS

Perfect for spring or summer, these muesli pots replace the traditional oats with wheat berries that add a delicious nutty flavor and texture.

SERVES 4 · PREP 25 MINS, PLUS OVERNIGHT SOAKING AND COOLING · COOK 30 MINS

⅔ cup uncooked wheat berries

9oz (250g) blueberries

9oz (250g) strawberries, hulled

1⅔ cups plain yogurt

¼ cup sunflower seeds, plus extra to serve

¼ cup honey, plus extra to serve

1 Place the wheat berries in a large bowl, cover with water, and leave to soak overnight or for up to 8 hours. Then drain well, rinse under running water, and drain again.

2 Place the wheat berries in a large saucepan, cover with plenty of water, and bring to a boil. Then reduce the heat to a simmer, cover, and cook for 30 minutes or until the wheat berries are tender. Remove from the heat, drain any remaining water, and leave to cool completely.

3 Meanwhile, wash the blueberries and place them in a separate bowl. Wash the strawberries and cut them into thin slices. Add them to the blueberries and toss to mix. Once cooled, place the wheat berries, yogurt, sunflower seeds, and honey in a large bowl. Mix until well combined.

4 Divide half the wheat berry and yogurt mixture equally between 4 serving bowls, glasses, or jars. Top with a layer of half the strawberries and blueberries. Repeat the process adding one more layer of yogurt and fruit. Sprinkle some sunflower seeds on top and add a drizzle of honey before serving.

GRAIN EXCHANGE

In place of the wheat berries, you could use any one of the following grains. Use the same amount as the wheat berries and see p16–17 for advice on cooking times.

buckwheat

kamut

farro

why not try...

Try adding **raspberries** and **blackberries** in place of the blueberries and strawberries.

BAKED BLUEBERRY AND SPELT OATMEAL

A healthy breakfast dish that feels like a treat. The spelt adds a nutty flavor and a crunchy, chewy texture to the oats that complement the sweet and savory mixture of soft fruit and mixed nuts.

SERVES 6 · PREP 15 MINS, PLUS COOLING · COOK 30-35 MINS

½ cup uncooked spelt

4 tsp extra virgin olive oil, plus extra for greasing

10oz (300g) blueberries

1½ cups rolled oats

1 tsp baking powder

¼ tsp ground cinnamon

¼ tsp grated nutmeg

pinch of salt

2 large eggs

2 cups whole milk or almond milk

1 tsp vanilla extract

3 tbsp maple syrup

2 tbsp mixed seeds, such as pumpkin, chia, and sunflower seeds

1 Place the spelt in a lidded saucepan, cover with 2 cups of water, and bring to a boil. Then reduce the heat to a simmer, cover, and cook for about 45 minutes, until most of the water has been absorbed. Remove from the heat, drain any remaining water, and rinse well under running water. Set aside to dry.

2 Preheat the oven to 350°F (180°C). Grease an 8 x10in (20 x 25cm) baking dish with a little oil. Spread out the blueberries in an even layer at the bottom of the dish. Place the oats, baking powder, cinnamon, nutmeg, and salt in a bowl. Add the spelt and mix until well combined. Place the eggs, milk, vanilla extract, maple syrup, and oil in a separate bowl and whisk to combine.

3 Add the wet mixture to the dry ingredients and mix until well combined. Spoon the mixture over the blueberries and spread it out in an even layer. Top with a layer of the mixed seeds and place in the oven. Bake for 30–35 minutes or until the top is golden brown and the oats are cooked. Remove from the heat and leave to cool slightly. Serve warm.

QUINOA AND POLENTA BREAKFAST MUFFINS
WITH FRIED EGGS, BACON, AND AVOCADO

Rich in whole grains, these deliciously savory muffins make a perfect start to your day. Serve the muffins with eggs, bacon, and avocado for a filling and hearty breakfast.

SERVES 4 · PREP 10 MINS · COOK 20 MINS

1 tbsp light olive oil

4 large eggs

8 bacon slices

1 tbsp butter, to serve

2 avocados, pitted and cut into thin slices

FOR THE BATTER

¾ cup polenta or corn grits

½ cup whole wheat flour

¾ cup prepared quinoa (see p22)

1 tbsp baking powder

½ tsp baking soda

¾ tsp sea salt

1 cup milk

3½ tbsp light olive oil

1 tbsp honey

3 large eggs

1 Preheat the oven to 400°F (200°C). Grease and line an 8-hole muffin pan with baking cups. For the batter, place the polenta, flour, quinoa, baking powder, baking soda, and salt in a large bowl and mix to combine.

2 In a separate bowl, whisk together the milk, oil, honey, and eggs until well combined. Then gently fold the liquid mixture into the dry ingredients and mix until just combined.

3 Divide the batter equally between the 8 baking cups and transfer the pan to the oven. Bake for about 20 minutes or until a toothpick inserted into the center comes out clean.

4 Meanwhile, heat the oil in a frying pan over medium heat and fry the eggs. Then add the bacon and fry until crisp. Split the muffins, top with some butter, and serve with the fried eggs, bacon, and avocado.

MiLLET AND TEFF SWEET POTATO WAFFLES
WiTH COCONUT YOGURT

The subtle combination of millet and teff flour creates fluffy, nutty waffles that are also gluten-free. The refreshing coconut milk yogurt neatly complements the tangy sweet potatoes, making this tasty breakfast dairy-free as well.

MAKES 12 · PREP 15 MINS, PLUS CHILLING · COOK 50–55 MINS

1 large sweet potato, about 14oz (400g), diced

1 tbsp olive oil

1 cup teff flour

½ cup millet flour

½ tsp salt

2 tsp baking powder

¼ tsp ground cinnamon

½ tsp grated nutmeg

¼ cup coconut oil, room temperature, plus extra for greasing

3 eggs, lightly beaten

1 tsp vanilla extract

3 tbsp maple syrup, plus extra to serve

14oz (400g) can coconut milk

1 tbsp shredded coconut, plus extra to serve

1 cup coconut milk yogurt

1 Preheat the oven to 400°F (200°C). Place the sweet potatoes on a small baking sheet and drizzle with the olive oil. Bake the sweet potatoes for about 30 minutes, until tender and cooked through. Remove from the heat and leave to cool. Once cooled, mash the potatoes with the back of a fork until smooth, then set aside.

2 Reduce the oven temperature to 250°F (130°C). Preheat the waffle maker or iron. Place both flours, salt, baking powder, cinnamon, and nutmeg in a large bowl and mix well. In a separate bowl, place the coconut oil, eggs, vanilla extract, maple syrup, coconut milk, and mashed potatoes. Mix until well combined.

3 Add the wet mixture to the dry ingredients and stir well until the mixture is smooth and well incorporated. Lightly grease the waffle maker. Pour a small ladleful of the batter onto the waffle maker or iron and spread almost to the edge. Close the lid and bake until golden brown. Transfer to the heated oven and keep warm in a single layer while you make the rest of the waffles.

4 Meanwhile, place the coconut and yogurt in a large bowl and mix well to combine. Cover with plastic wrap and chill in the fridge for about 15 minutes. Place warm waffles on plates and top with a scoop of the yogurt. Sprinkle some shredded coconut over them, drizzle with maple syrup, and serve immediately.

SOAKED BUCKWHEAT PANCAKES
WiTH CHERRY ALMOND SAUCE

Buckwheat makes an incredible gluten-free flour and is even kinder on your digestion when soaked overnight. These fluffy and wholesome pancakes are perfectly paired with a cherry almond sauce.

MAKES 8 PANCAKES · PREP 10 MiNS, PLUS OVERNiGHT SOAKiNG · COOK 30 MiNS

FOR THE BATTER

1¼ cups buckwheat flour

¼ cup plain yogurt

¾ cup milk

2 eggs

¾ tsp baking soda

¼ tsp baking powder

½ tsp vanilla extract

⅛ tsp salt

1–2 tbsp coconut oil, plus extra if needed

Greek yogurt, to serve

FOR THE SAUCE

12oz (350g) cherries, pitted

3 tbsp sugar

1 tsp almond extract

1 For the batter, place the flour, yogurt, and milk in a large bowl. Mix to combine, cover with a paper towel, and leave at room temperature for 8 hours or up to 24 hours.

2 Place the eggs, baking soda, baking powder, vanilla, and salt in a large bowl. Whisk lightly until well blended. Then gradually pour the egg mixture into the flour mixture and whisk until well combined.

3 Heat a large nonstick frying pan over medium-high heat and add the oil once the pan is hot. Pour tablespoons of the batter into the pan, leaving space between them for the pancakes to spread. Each pancake should spread to about 6in (15cm) in diameter.

4 Cook the pancakes until small bubbles appear on the surface and the underside is firm. Then turn them over and cook for another 1–2 minutes or until cooked through. Transfer the cooked pancakes to a warm oven. Continue cooking until all the batter is used up, adding more oil to the pan as needed.

5 For the sauce, place the cherries in a large, lidded saucepan and cover with ½ cup of water. Add the sugar and place the pan over medium-high heat. Cover and simmer until the cherries have broken down. Then uncover and cook until the liquid becomes syrupy. Remove from the heat and stir in the almond extract. Serve the cherry almond sauce with the pancakes and Greek yogurt.

CRANBERRY, ORANGE, AND CHOCOLATE QUiNOA BARS

The perfect breakfast on the go or handy snack, these sweet, chewy, and wholesome bars feel like a treat, but pack a big nutritional punch and will keep you full all morning.

MAKES 12 BARS · PREP 20 MiNS, PLUS COOLING · COOK 5 MiNS

1 cup almonds, coarsely chopped

3 cups quinoa flakes

¾ cup sunflower seeds

¾ cup chia seeds

⅔ cup dried cranberries

6 cups puffed rice cereal

1¾oz (50g) dark chocolate chips

grated zest of 2 large oranges

⅓ cup coconut oil

½ cup honey

¼ cup brown sugar

1 Place the almonds, quinoa flakes, sunflower seeds, chia seeds, dried cranberries, puffed rice cereal, chocolate chips, and orange zest in a bowl. Mix well with a wooden spoon and set aside. Grease and line an 8 x 10in (20 x 25cm) baking pan with parchment paper.

2 Heat the oil, honey, and sugar in a saucepan over medium heat. Cook, stirring occasionally, for about 5 minutes or until the sugar has melted and the mixture is bubbling. Set aside to cool for about 2 minutes.

3 Pour the cooled honey mixture into the dry ingredients. Mix using a wooden spoon until well incorporated, making sure the chocolate chips have melted and are evenly combined. Spoon the mixture into the prepared baking pan. Press down firmly with the back of a wooden spoon to make a roughly even layer.

4 Place the baking pan in the fridge for at least 4 hours to allow the mixture to cool and harden. Remove from the fridge, turn out on to a cutting board, and cut into bars. These can be stored in an airtight container in the fridge for up to 5 days.

GRAIN EXCHANGE

If you don't have quinoa flakes, then try using the same amount of **millet flakes** instead.

why not try...

Add **walnuts** instead of the almonds, **pumpkin seeds** instead of sunflower seeds, and **raisins** or **chopped dates** instead of the cranberries. In each case, use the same amount of the substitute ingredient as recommended in the recipe.

STRAWBERRY BARLEY SCONES

This British classic is given a whole grain twist with the addition of barley. Use other berries instead of strawberries, depending on the season.

MAKES 8 · PREP 20 MINS, PLUS COOLING · COOK 20 MINS

1 cup barley flour

1¼ cups whole wheat all-purpose flour, plus extra for dusting

½ tsp salt

1 tbsp baking powder

½ tsp baking soda

½ cup unsalted butter, chilled and diced

4½oz (125g) strawberries, finely chopped

1 tsp vanilla extract

1 large egg

⅓ cup whole milk, plus extra for brushing

¼ cup maple syrup

1 tbsp cane sugar

1 Preheat the oven to 400°F (200°C). Line a baking sheet with parchment paper. Place both types of flour, the salt, baking powder, and baking soda in a large bowl. Mix well to combine. Then rub in the butter until the mixture resembles bread crumbs. Add the strawberries and mix well.

2 Place the vanilla extract, egg, milk, and maple syrup in a separate bowl and whisk to combine. Add the wet mixture to the dry ingredients and mix until just combined. Be careful not to overmix.

3 On a well-floured surface, roll out the dough to a ½in (1cm) thick square, roughly 7in (18cm) in size. Then cut the dough into four equal-sized squares. Cut the squares diagonally, to form triangles, and transfer to the prepared baking sheet.

4 Brush the scones with milk, sprinkle the tops with sugar, and bake for 18–20 minutes, until turning golden. Remove from the heat and leave to cool on the baking sheet for 10 minutes. Then transfer to a wire rack to cool. Serve at room temperature.

CARAMELIZED AMARANTH PORRIDGE

Start the day off right, with a warm bowl of sweet porridge topped with syrupy caramelized bananas.

SERVES 4 · PREP 10 MINS · COOK 30 MINS

1 cup uncooked amaranth

⅓ cup sugar

3 ripe bananas, halved lengthwise and sliced into ½in (1cm) pieces

2 tbsp brown sugar

1 tsp lemon juice

1 tsp ground cinnamon

pinch of rock salt

1 tbsp unsalted butter

1 Place 2¾ cups of water in a large, lidded saucepan and bring to a boil. Add the amaranth, cover, and reduce the heat to medium-low. Cook for about 20 minutes or until all the water has been absorbed. Add the sugar, mix well to combine, and remove from the heat.

2 Meanwhile, place the bananas, brown sugar, lemon juice, cinnamon, and salt in a large bowl. Mix gently to coat the bananas and form a syrupy mixture.

3 Melt the butter in a nonstick frying pan, swirling to coat the bottom. When the butter begins to bubble, add the banana mixture and cook, stirring occasionally, for 3–4 minutes or until the bananas are softened and begin to turn golden. Remove from the heat. Divide the amaranth between four bowls and top with the caramelized bananas. Serve immediately.

SORGHUM AND EGGS RANCHERO

This popular Mexican breakfast is given a hearty and healthy touch with the use of the nutrient-rich super-grain sorghum in place of the more usual rice. The spicy salsa and salty Manchego cheese are the perfect accompaniments.

SERVES 4 · PREP 10 MINS, PLUS STANDING · COOK 1 HR

½ cup uncooked sorghum

2 cups chicken stock

3 tbsp extra virgin olive oil, plus extra if needed

14oz (400g) can black beans, drained and rinsed

½ teaspoon cumin

4 small corn tortillas

4 large eggs

2 avocados, pitted and diced

⅓ cup Manchego cheese

handful of cilantro, coarsely chopped

FOR THE SALSA

3 tomatoes, grated

2–3 tbsp finely chopped onion

1 jalapeño, finely chopped

1 garlic clove, crushed

1–2 tbsp hot sauce

salt and freshly ground black pepper

1 Place the sorghum in a small saucepan, cover with the stock, and bring to a boil. Then reduce the heat to a simmer, cover, and cook for 45 minutes. Remove from the heat and leave to stand, covered, for about 10 minutes. Then drain any remaining water and set aside.

2 Meanwhile, for the salsa, place the tomatoes, onions, jalapeños, garlic, and hot sauce in a bowl. Season with a pinch of salt and some pepper and mix well. Heat 2 tablespoons of the oil in a small saucepan over medium-low heat. Add the tomato mixture and cook for 2–3 minutes, until thickened and well combined. Remove from the heat and set aside.

3 In a separate pan, add the beans, cumin, and 3 tablespoons of water. Cook over medium heat, stirring occasionally, until most of the water has evaporated and the beans are tender. Remove from the heat and coarsely mash the beans with the back of a fork. Set aside.

4 Heat a large frying pan over medium-low heat. Add the tortillas and warm through for about 2 minutes on each side. Remove from the heat and set aside. Wipe the pan with paper towels, add the remaining oil, and increase the heat to medium. Fry the eggs, one at a time, adding more oil to the pan if needed.

5 To assemble the dish, divide the tortillas between four serving plates. Top with equal quantities of the sorghum and one fried egg each. Divide the beans, salsa, and avocado equally between the plates. Sprinkle over the Manchego cheese, garnish with cilantro, and serve immediately.

tomatoes

BACON, CHEESE, AND KÁMUT FRÍTTATA

A hearty and filling portion in every slice, this traditional italian omelette is really nutritious and is given a brand new feel and taste with the inclusion of super-food kamut.

SERVES 4–6 · PREP 20 MINS · COOK 30 MINS

1 onion, finely chopped

6 bacon slices, cut into bite-sized pieces

8oz (225g) spinach, coarsely chopped

6 large eggs

1 cup freshly grated medium Cheddar cheese

1 cup prepared kamut (see p22)

salt and freshly ground black pepper

1 Heat a large nonstick, ovenproof frying pan over medium-high heat. Add the onions and bacon and cook for about 5 minutes, until the bacon is cooked and the onions are translucent.

2 Add the spinach to the pan and cook for about 5 minutes, until it wilts and reduces in volume. Remove from the heat and set aside.

3 Place the eggs and cheese in a large bowl and whisk to combine. Add the kamut to the egg mixture and mix to combine. Then add the bacon and spinach mixture to the bowl and season. Whisk lightly to ensure that all the ingredients are well combined.

4 Return the pan to the stove and place over medium-low heat. Pour the frittata mixture into the pan and cook for 10–15 minutes, without moving it, until the edges are set and the underside is cooked.

5 Set the broiler at its highest setting and allow it to heat up for 5 minutes. Then place the pan under the broiler for 2–3 minutes, until the frittata is golden brown on top. Remove from the heat and leave to rest for about 5 minutes. Slice into wedges and serve warm or at room temperature.

GRAIN EXCHANGE

This dish works well with a variety of similar grains. Try replacing the kamut with the same amount of any of the following.

wheat berries

spelt

farro

why not try...

Use the same amount of **broccoli** in place of spinach. You can use it parboiled and drained or finely chopped and lightly sautéed.

MiLLET, BANANA, AND WALNUT BREAD

Sweet and bursting with fruit flavor, this banana bread benefits from the added millet, which provides it with a crunchy, nutty texture, as well as whole-grain goodness.

MAKES 2LB (900G) LOAF · PREP 20 MiNS · COOK 1 HR

2 cups whole wheat flour

½ cup brown sugar

1 tsp baking soda

½ tsp baking powder

½ tsp cinnamon

⅔ cup walnuts, chopped

¼ tsp salt

2 bananas

2 large eggs

¼ cup olive oil, plus extra for greasing

¼ cup plain yogurt

¾ cup prepared millet (see p22)

1 Preheat the oven to 350°F (180°C). Grease and line a 2lb (900g) loaf pan with parchment paper. Place the flour, sugar, baking soda, baking powder, cinnamon, walnuts, and salt in a bowl and mix well.

2 Place the bananas in a separate bowl and mash with a fork. Add the eggs, oil, and yogurt and mix until well incorporated. Then add the millet to the banana mixture and mix gently until combined.

3 Gradually fold the flour mixture into the banana and millet mixture until just combined. If the batter is over-mixed, the bread will be tough. Spoon the batter into the loaf pan and transfer to the oven.

4 Bake for 40 minutes, then remove from the oven and cover with foil. Return to the oven for another 20 minutes or until a skewer inserted into the center of the loaf comes out clean. Remove from the oven and leave to cool completely before serving.

GRAiN EXCHANGE

For a change, you could use the same amount of prepared **quinoa** in place of the millet.

why not try...

Try adding the same amount of **pecans** in place of the walnuts. You can also try using ⅔ cup of **coconut palm sugar** instead of the brown sugar.

HAM AND CHEESE EGG SCRAMBLE WITH VEGETABLE FARRO HASH

Simple to make, these classic scrambled eggs with ham and cheese get an extra vibrancy from the vegetables and farro, making it a complete meal that is perfect for a leisurely family breakfast.

SERVES 4 · PREP 10 MiNS · COOK 20 MiNS

2 tbsp olive oil

1 red onion, diced

7oz (200g) zucchini, diced

1 red bell pepper, seeded and diced

¾ cup prepared farro (see p22)

¼ cup basil coarsely chopped

salt and freshly ground black pepper

4 large eggs

¼ cup milk

1 tbsp butter

4oz (115g) cooked ham, diced

1 cup freshly grated Cheddar cheese

1 Heat the oil in a large frying pan over medium heat. Add the onions, zucchini, and red bell pepper. Cook for 8–10 minutes, stirring occasionally, until the vegetables are softened. Then add the farro and basil and stir to mix. Cook, stirring frequently, for another 2 minutes or until heated through. Season to taste and remove from the heat. Set aside and keep warm.

2 Meanwhile, place the eggs and milk in a large bowl. Season with salt and pepper and whisk well to combine. Heat the butter in a nonstick frying pan over medium heat. Pour in the egg mixture and cook, stirring occasionally, until cooked through. Then add the ham and cheese, stir to combine, and remove from the heat. Divide the egg scramble and vegetable farro hash equally between four plates and serve hot.

basil

PUMPKIN SPICED TEFF PORRIDGE

This rich spiced porridge made with teff is like fall in a bowl—don't just save it for Halloween!

SERVES 2 · PREP 5 MINS · COOK 20 MINS

½ cup uncooked teff	1 tsp ground cinnamon
7oz (200g) pumpkin purée	½ tsp ground ginger
½ cup milk	¼ cup pecans
¼ cup maple syrup	

1 Place the teff and 1⅔ cups of water in a large saucepan over medium-high heat. Bring to a simmer and cook for about 15 minutes, stirring frequently, until all the water has been absorbed and the teff has a thick oatmeal-like consistency. Remove from the heat

2 Add the pumpkin purée, milk, maple syrup, cinnamon, and ginger. Mix well and return to medium heat. Cook the porridge for 2 minutes, stirring constantly, until warmed through and well combined. Remove from the heat and sprinkle with the pecans. Serve hot.

SPELT BERRY BREAKFAST SALAD

Something a bit different for breakfast, this light salad is full of flavor matched with creamy Greek yogurt.

SERVES 4 · PREP 10 MINS · COOK 40 MINS

½ cup uncooked spelt	honey, to serve
3½oz (100g) blackberries	Greek yogurt, to serve
3½oz (100g) raspberries	
¼ cup coarsely chopped mint	

1 Place the spelt in a large saucepan, cover with plenty of water, and bring to a boil. Then reduce the heat to a simmer and cook for 30–40 minutes, until tender. Remove from the heat and drain any remaining water. Rinse the spelt under running cold water.

2 Place the spelt in a bowl. Add the blackberries, raspberries, and mint. Mix well to combine. Divide the salad between bowls and top with the honey. Serve immediately with Greek yogurt.

BLUEBERRY, AMARANTH, AND VANILLA MUFFINS

These tender breakfast muffins are made with nutty wholesome amaranth and dotted with ripe, sweet blueberries. Perfect when served warm with your morning coffee or even a glass of juice.

MAKES 12 MUFFINS · PREP 10 MINS · COOK 50 MINS

¼ cup uncooked amaranth

1 large egg

1 cup half and half

½ cup canola oil, plus extra for greasing

2 cups all-purpose flour

⅓ cup granulated sugar

1 tbsp baking powder

½ tsp salt

1 tsp vanilla extract

8oz (225g) blueberries

1 Place the amaranth in a large saucepan, cover with water, and cook according to package instructions. Remove from the heat, drain any remaining water, and leave to cool. Preheat the oven to 400°F (200°C). Grease and line a 12-hole muffin pan with baking cups.

2 Place the egg, half and half, and oil in a large bowl and beat together until combined. Add the flour, sugar, baking powder, salt, and vanilla extract to the mixture. Mix well to combine. Then add the blueberries and cooled amaranth and mix until evenly incorporated.

3 Divide the batter evenly between the baking cups. Transfer to the oven and bake for 25–30 minutes, until golden brown on top and a skewer inserted into the middle comes out clean. Leave the muffins in the pan to cool for 10 minutes. Then transfer to a wire rack to cool slightly. Serve warm.

GRAIN EXCHANGE

As an alternative, use the same amount of **quinoa** in place of the amaranth and cook it for 15 minutes.

why not try...

Instead of blueberries, try adding the same amount of **raspberries** or **dried cranberries**.

APPLE AND CiNNAMON BREAKFAST FREEKEH

Crisp and tart apples and sweet apple juice combine with tender freekeh for a delicious and warming breakfast.

SERVES 4 · PREP 5 MiNS · COOK 20 MiNS

2½ cups apple juice	2 tbsp brown sugar
¾ cup cracked freekeh	ground cinnamon, to taste
1 Granny Smith apple, cored and diced	

1 Place the apple juice, freekeh, and apple pieces in a large saucepan. Mix well, set the pan over medium heat, and bring to a boil.

2 Reduce the heat to medium-low, cover, and cook for 15–20 minutes, stirring occasionally, until the freekeh is tender.

3 Remove from the heat, stir in the sugar, and mix well to combine. Then add the cinnamon, as desired, and serve immediately.

CHOCOLATE AND HAZELNUT GRANOLA

For the sweet-toothed, this delicious variation on granola is the perfect start to the day.

MAKES ABOUT 1³/₄LB (800G) · PREP 15 MiNS · COOK 15 MiNS

½ cup honey	¼ cup pumpkin seeds
⅓ cup coconut oil	¼ cup sunflower seeds
⅓ cup cocoa powder	¾ cup hazelnuts, coarsely chopped
½ tsp salt	
1¼ cups oats	
1¼ cups prepared buckwheat (see p22)	

1 Preheat the oven to 350°F (180°C). Line two baking sheets with parchment paper and set aside. Place the honey in a large bowl. Melt the oil over a bowl of warm water and add to the honey. Then add the cocoa powder and salt to the bowl and mix well to combine.

2 Place the oats, buckwheat, pumpkin seeds, sunflower seeds, and hazelnuts in a separate bowl and mix to combine. Then add the honey, oil, and cocoa powder mixture to the dry ingredients and mix until well incorporated.

3 Divide the mixture evenly between the baking sheets and spread it out to form a thin layer. Place in the oven and bake for 15 minutes. Remove from the oven and taste a little of the mixture to check if it is well toasted. Leave to cool on the sheet. Serve with plain yogurt or fresh soft fruit.

BUCKWHEAT CRÊPES
WITH BRIE, APPLE, WALNUTS, AND PROSCIUTTO

These crêpes are based on the traditional Breton galette. The combination of fruit, cheese, and salty meat is a great blend of flavors and textures.

SERVES 4 · PREP 10 MINS · COOK 20 MINS

1–2 tbsp unsalted butter, room temperature, plus extra if needed

1 apple, thinly sliced

1½ cups Brie cheese, cut into small pieces

½ cup walnuts, coarsely chopped

4 slices prosciutto, roughly chopped

FOR THE BATTER

1 tbsp unsalted butter, melted

2/3 cup buckwheat flour

2/3 cup whole milk

2 large eggs

1 Heat 1 tablespoon of the butter in a frying pan. Add the apples and cook for about 2 minutes, turning them over occasionally, until softened and lightly browned on both sides. Remove from the heat. Set aside and keep warm.

2 For the batter, place all the ingredients in a food processor and pulse until combined. Heat the remaining butter in a large, nonstick frying pan over medium heat. Ladle 2–3 tablespoons of the batter into the center of the pan. Tip the pan or use the back of the ladle to swirl the batter to coat the bottom of the pan and form a thin layer.

3 Cook the crêpe for 2 minutes or until the edges start to curl up and it is crisp and lightly browned underneath. Flip the crêpe over, top with one-quarter of the Brie, and cook for 1–2 minutes. Remove from the heat, transfer to a plate, and keep warm.

4 Repeat with the remaining batter, adding more butter to the pan if needed. Place the crêpes on serving plates and top each with one-quarter of the apples, walnuts, and prosciutto. Then fold them in half, tuck in the sides, and serve warm.

apple

SPINACH AND ARTICHOKE QUICHE WITH AN AMARANTH CRUST

This tasty quiche uses amaranth flour for a delicious gluten-free and vegan crust and is ideal for a healthy and filling brunch. For best results, use artichokes that have been preserved in oil instead of canned in water or brine.

SERVES 6 · PREP 20 MINS · COOK 50 MINS

FOR THE PASTRY

½ cup amaranth flour

¼ cup ground almonds

¼ tsp salt

⅓ cup tapioca flour
   or cornstarch

3 tbsp vegetable oil

FOR THE FILLING

1 tbsp olive oil

1 garlic clove, crushed

¾ cup onion, finely chopped

5oz (140g) spinach

4–5 artichoke hearts, drained
   and roughly chopped

2oz (60g) goat cheese

FOR THE CUSTARD

2 large eggs

2 egg yolks

1 cup whole milk

salt and freshly ground
   black pepper

1 Preheat the oven to 400°F (200°C). Grease a 9in (22cm) loose-bottomed tart pan and set aside. For the pastry, place the flour, almonds, salt, and flour, in a large bowl and mix well until combined. In a small bowl, whisk together the oil and 3 tablespoons of water. Make a well in the center of the dry ingredients and pour the oil mixture in. Bring together to form a light and sticky dough, adding more water, a little at a time, if needed.

2 Roll out the dough between two sheets of plastic wrap and use to line the prepared pan, making sure it forms a good side to the pan. Prick the bottom of the pastry with a fork. Place in the oven and blind bake for about 10 minutes. Then remove from the heat and set aside. Reduce the oven temperature to 350°F (180°C).

3 For the filling, heat the oil in a large saucepan over medium heat. Add the garlic and onions and cook for about 3–5 minutes or until the onions are translucent. Then add the spinach and cook for another 2–3 minutes or until it has wilted. Remove from the heat and set aside.

4 For the custard, place the eggs, yolks, and milk in a large bowl. Season with ¼ teaspoon salt and a good grinding of pepper. Whisk until well combined. Spoon the onion and spinach mixture into the pastry case, making sure it covers the bottom. Spread out the artichoke hearts on top in a single layer and pour over the custard. Crumble the goat cheese and sprinkle it over the custard.

5 Bake the quiche in the oven for about 40 minutes or until the custard has set and the top is golden. Remove from the heat and leave to cool slightly before cutting into wedges to serve. This quiche can be served warm or at room temperature.

NUTRiTiOUS
SOUPS

BEET AND BUCKWHEAT SOUP
WITH LEMON YOGURT SAUCE

A vibrant and soothing soup, the contrasting flavors of the beet and tangy yogurt sauce are perfectly paired with the buckwheat for an ideal lunch or light dinner.

SERVES 4 · PREP 15 MINS · COOK 50 MINS

1 tbsp light olive oil

1 onion, finely chopped

1lb 10oz (750g) beets, trimmed and cut into small chunks

2 cups vegetable stock

14oz (400g) can chopped tomatoes

salt and freshly ground black pepper

1 cup prepared buckwheat (see p22)

handful of rosemary leaves

FOR THE SAUCE

1 cup plain yogurt

juice of 1 lemon

1 Heat the oil in a large saucepan over medium heat. Add the onion and cook for about 5 minutes, stirring frequently, until translucent. Then add the beets and stock. Bring the mixture to a simmer and cook for 30–40 minutes, until the beets are tender.

2 Add the tomatoes to the pan and cook for 2–3 minutes. Transfer the soup to a food processor and pulse until it reaches a smooth consistency. Season to taste, if needed. Pour the soup back into the pan and heat through over low heat for 2–3 minutes. Remove from the heat.

3 For the sauce, place the ingredients in a bowl and mix to combine. Divide the soup between four bowls and top with the sauce. Then add equal quantities of the buckwheat, garnish with rosemary, and serve hot.

GRAIN EXCHANGE

Try replacing the buckwheat with the same amount of prepared sorghum or millet.

millet

sorghum

CREAMY GREEN SOUP WITH WHEAT BERRIES

This gorgeous green soup is made extra creamy with the dairy-free addition of cannellini beans. The wholesome wheat berries give this soup an added heartiness and texture.

SERVES 4 · PREP 15 MINS · COOK 30 MINS

- 1 tbsp olive oil
- 1 onion, finely chopped
- 2 garlic cloves, crushed
- 4 leeks, trimmed and finely sliced
- 1lb 2oz (500g) spring greens, stems removed and finely sliced
- 3 cups vegetable stock
- 2 x 14oz (400g) can cooked cannellini beans, drained
- salt and freshly ground black pepper
- 2⅓ cups prepared and cooled wheat berries (see p22)

1 Heat the oil in a large saucepan over medium heat. Add the onions and garlic and cook, stirring occasionally, for about 5 minutes.

2 Add the leeks to the pan and cook for about 10 minutes, stirring occasionally, until softened. Then add the spring greens and cook for another 2–3 minutes or until they wilt.

3 Pour in the vegetable stock, bring the soup to a boil, and allow to simmer for about 10 minutes. Then add the cannellini beans to the pan and stir lightly to mix. Transfer the soup to a food processor and pulse until it reaches a smooth consistency. Season to taste, if needed.

4 Return the soup to the pan and place over medium heat for 2–3 minutes to heat through. Then stir in the wheat berries and remove from the heat. Ladle into soup bowls, season with pepper, and serve hot.

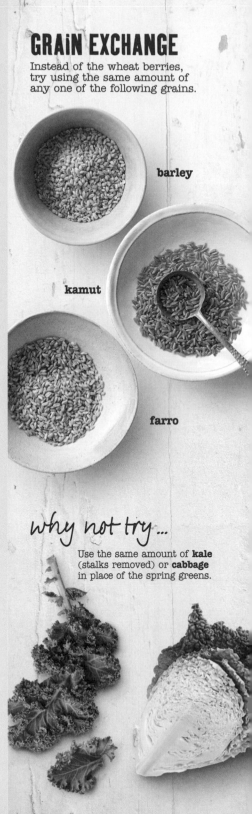

GRAIN EXCHANGE

Instead of the wheat berries, try using the same amount of any one of the following grains.

barley

kamut

farro

why not try...

Use the same amount of **kale** (stalks removed) or **cabbage** in place of the spring greens.

SPRING VEGETABLE AND SORGHUM MINESTRONE
WITH PESTO

This refreshing soup is also full of goodness. Packed with flavor, it makes the best of fresh spring vegetables and wholesome sorghum and can be enjoyed on a warm or cool day alike.

SERVES 4 · PREP 15 MINS · COOK 1 HR 25 MINS

¼ cup extra virgin olive oil

1 small fennel bulb, white and green parts only, diced

1 scallion, diced

6 garlic cloves, thinly sliced

1 white potato, diced

1 tsp dried thyme

¼ tsp chile flakes (optional)

salt and freshly ground black pepper

½ cup uncooked sorghum

14oz (400g) can cannellini beans, drained

3½oz (100g) leafy greens, such as kale, spinach, and bok choy

FOR THE PESTO

large bunch of basil

1 small garlic clove, crushed

⅓ cup toasted pine nuts

½ cup freshly grated Parmesan cheese

½ cup extra virgin olive oil

1 Heat the oil in a large, heavy-bottomed soup pot over medium heat. Add the fennel and onions and cook for 10 minutes or until softened. Then add the garlic, potatoes, thyme, and chile flakes. Season with ½ teaspoon salt, stir to mix, and cook for another 2–3 minutes.

2 Add the sorghum and pour in 2 quarts of water. Bring to a boil, then reduce the heat to a simmer. Cook for about 40 minutes. Then add the beans, stir to mix, and cook for another 20 minutes. Season to taste and cook for another 2 minutes if the soup seems too watery. Add the greens, stir well, and cook for 5 minutes or until they have just about wilted. Remove from the heat.

3 For the pesto, place all the ingredients, except the oil, in a food processor. Pulse until roughly chopped and well combined. Then add the oil in a slow stream and pulse until emulsified. Taste, adding seasoning, if needed. Ladle the soup into bowls and top with a spoonful of pesto. Serve hot.

SUMMER PEA, MINT, AND AVOCADO SOUP WITH QUINOA

This light and creamy chilled soup is enhanced with the addition of the nutty flavored and protein-packed quinoa. Quick and easy to prepare, it makes the perfect summer lunch.

SERVES 4 · PREP 10 MINS · COOK 25 MINS

⅓ cup uncooked quinoa

2 avocados, pitted

1lb 2oz (500g) frozen peas

¾ cup chopped mint, plus extra to garnish

1 quart unsweetened almond milk

1 Rinse the quinoa under running water, drain, and place in a lidded saucepan. Cover with 1 cup of water and bring to a boil.

2 Reduce the heat to a simmer, cover, and cook for 15–20 minutes or until almost all the liquid has been absorbed and the quinoa is fluffy. Remove from the heat, drain any remaining water, and set aside to cool.

3 Scoop out the flesh from the avocados and place in a food processor. Add the peas, mint, and half the milk and pulse until smooth. Then add the remaining milk and pulse until fully incorporated.

4 Divide the soup equally between four soup bowls. Top with equal quantities of the cooled quinoa. Garnish with some mint and serve immediately.

GRAIN EXCHANGE

You could use the same amount of barley or spelt in place of the quinoa.

barley

spelt

ROASTED TOMATO AND RED PEPPER SOUP WiTH FARRO

This tangy version of the classic tomato soup is given a nutritional boost with the use of farro.

SERVES 4 · PREP 15 MiNS, PLUS SOAKiNG · COOK 1 HR 10 MiNS

¾ cup uncooked farro

1¾lb (800g) tomatoes, quartered

3 red bell peppers, seeded and coarsely chopped

1 onion, coarsely chopped

4 garlic cloves, crushed

3 tbsp olive oil

2 cups vegetable stock

salt and freshly ground black pepper

¼ cup chopped basil

1 Place the farro in a large bowl, cover with water, and leave to soak for 8 hours or for up to 12 hours. Then drain, rinse under running water, and drain well again. Place the farro in a saucepan and cover with water. Bring to a boil, then reduce the heat to a simmer, and cook for 30 minutes or until tender, but still with some bite. Remove from the heat.

2 Preheat the oven to 350°F (180°C). Place the tomatoes, red bell peppers, onions, and garlic in a baking sheet, drizzle the oil over them, and toss to coat. Place the sheet in the oven and roast the vegetables for 45 minutes or until soft and slightly caramelized. Remove from the heat.

3 Transfer the vegetable mixture, along with any juices in the pan, to a food processor and pulse until smooth. Then add the stock, a little at a time, and pulse until it is well combined and reaches a soup-like consistency. Pour the soup into a pan and place over low heat. Add the farro, stir to mix, and heat through for about 5 minutes. Season to taste, garnish with basil, and serve warm.

CHiPOTLE SWEET POTATO SOUP

Creamy and rich sweet potatoes and chipotle chiles are perfectly combined for a spicy twist to this popular soup.

SERVES 4 · PREP 10 MiNS · COOK 1 HR 10 MiNS

1 tbsp olive oil

1 sweet onion, diced

2 garlic cloves, crushed

2 chipotle chiles in 2 tbsp adobo sauce, finely chopped

1 quart low-sodium vegetable stock

1lb (450g) sweet potatoes, cut into 1in (2.5cm) cubes

1 tbsp honey

⅓ cup uncooked freekeh

salt and freshly ground black pepper

1 Heat the oil in a Dutch oven or a large casserole over medium heat. Add the onions and garlic and sauté for 3–5 minutes or until the onions are lightly browned. Then stir in the chipotle chiles and adobo sauce. Mix well to combine.

2 Add the stock, sweet potatoes, and honey. Stir to mix and bring the mixture to a boil. Then reduce the heat to medium-low, cover, and cook for about 30 minutes. Remove from the heat.

3 Use a handheld blender to process the mixture to a purée. Stir in the freekeh and place over medium-low heat and cook, stirring occasionally, for another 30 minutes. Remove from the heat. Season to taste and serve immediately.

CREAMY MUSHROOM BARLEY SOUP

Keep some dried mushrooms and barley in your pantry so you can prepare this easy soup without much effort. Bursting with the flavors of dried herbs and white wine, it is filling enough to eat on its own and is an excellent winter soup.

SERVES 4–6 · PREP 10 MINS, PLUS SOAKING · COOK 1 HR

1oz (30g) mixed, dried porcini and shiitake mushrooms

½ cup uncooked barley

pinch of salt

1 tbsp unsalted butter

2 tbsp olive oil

1 onion, diced

2 garlic cloves, crushed

1 tsp dried thyme

1 tsp dried rosemary

½ tsp sea salt

6½oz (190g) cremini mushrooms, thinly sliced lengthwise

6½fl oz (190ml) dry white wine

1 quart low-sodium chicken stock

2 tbsp all-purpose flour

⅔ cup Greek yogurt, room temperature

1 tbsp coarsely chopped chives, to garnish

1 Place the dried mushrooms in a large bowl and cover with 2 cups of warm water. Leave to soak for 30 minutes. Then drain the mushrooms and reserve the water. Coarsely chop the mushrooms and set aside.

2 Place the barley in a large, lidded saucepan and cover with 1½ cups of water. Add a pinch of salt and bring to a boil. Then reduce the heat to a simmer, cover, and cook for 45 minutes or until the barley is tender and all the liquid has been absorbed. Remove from the heat. Cover and set aside.

3 Meanwhile, heat the butter and oil in a large, heavy-bottomed pot over medium heat. Add the onions and cook for 2–3 minutes, stirring frequently, until soft and translucent. Then add the garlic, thyme, rosemary, and sea salt and stir to mix. Cook, stirring frequently, for another 2 minutes.

4 Add the porcini, shiitake, and cremini mushrooms. Cook, stirring frequently, for about 5 minutes or until the mushrooms have softened and are starting to brown. Then add the wine, stir to coat, and cook for about 10 minutes until it has evaporated.

5 Add the stock to the pot and stir to mix. Bring to a boil, then reduce the heat to a simmer, and cook for 5 minutes. Transfer ½ cup of the liquid to a bowl. Add the flour and whisk until well combined and smooth. Pour the mixture back into the soup, stir to combine, and cook for another 20–25 minutes.

6 Add in the barley and cook, stirring occasionally, for 5 minutes. Remove from the heat. Place the yogurt in a bowl and pour over 1 tablespoon of the soup. Mix well to combine and stir into the soup. Mix until evenly incorporated. Garnish with chives and serve warm.

SWEET POTATO AND PEANUT SOUP WITH TEFF

This sweet and spicy soup contains a hint of peanut and is inspired by the flavors of West African cuisine. The addition of teff gives the dish a light, earthy flavor and a unique texture.

SERVES 6–8 · PREP 15 MINS · COOK 45 MINS

½ cup uncooked teff

1 tbsp olive oil

1 onion, finely chopped

2 garlic cloves, finely chopped

1 tbsp ground cumin

14oz (400g) can chopped tomatoes

1lb 8oz (700g) sweet potatoes, unpeeled and cut into cubes

1 quart vegetable stock

⅓ cup smooth peanut butter

salt and freshly ground black pepper

1 cup plain yogurt, to serve

6 tbsp roughly chopped cilantro leaves, to serve

1 Place 1⅔ cups of water in a large saucepan and bring to a boil. Add the teff and reduce the heat to a simmer. Cook for 10 minutes, stirring constantly, until all the water has been absorbed. Then remove from the heat and set aside.

2 Meanwhile, heat the oil in a large saucepan over medium heat. Add the onions and garlic and sauté for about 5 minutes or until the onions have softened. Then add the cumin and sauté for another 2 minutes.

3 Add the tomatoes, sweet potatoes, and stock to the pan and reduce the heat to a simmer. Cover and cook for 30 minutes or until the potatoes are soft. Remove from the heat and use a handheld blender to process the soup until smooth. Then add the peanut butter and process until fully incorporated.

4 Add the teff to the soup and stir through. Return the pan to medium heat and warm through for 2–3 minutes. Remove from the heat and season to taste, if needed. Ladle into soup bowls and top with a spoonful of yogurt. Sprinkle over the cilantro and serve hot.

CHUNKY BUTTERNUT SQUASH AND BARLEY SOUP

The sweet and earthy flavor of orange–fleshed butternut squash shines through in this chunky soup, pepped up by just a hint of ginger and cinnamon. You can enjoy a bowl of this warming soup on the chilliest of fall days.

SERVES 4 · PREP 10 MINS · COOK 50 MINS

½ cup uncooked pearl barley

2 tbsp olive oil

1 onion, diced

salt and freshly ground black pepper

2 carrots, sliced into thin rounds

1 apple, cored and diced

1 red bell pepper, seeded and diced

1 butternut squash, about 2lb (900g), seeded and cut into cubes

1 quart vegetable stock

1 tsp ground cinnamon

1 tsp ground ginger

1 tsp paprika

1 Place the barley in a large saucepan, cover with 1½ cups of water, and bring to a boil. Reduce the heat to medium-low and cook for 25–30 minutes, or until tender. Then remove from the heat and drain any remaining water. Set aside.

2 Meanwhile, heat the olive oil in a large Dutch oven or saucepan over medium heat. Add the onions and season with a pinch of salt. Cook for about 8 minutes, stirring frequently, until they start to get translucent. Then add the carrots, apples, red bell pepper, and butternut squash. Stir to mix and pour in the vegetable stock. Cover and cook, stirring occasionally, for about 30 minutes.

3 Add the cinnamon, ginger, and paprika. Cook for another 10 minutes. Remove from the heat and take out about 5½oz (150g) of the vegetables with a slotted spoon and set aside. Use a handheld blender to pulse the remaining mixture until it forms a smooth purée. Add the barley and reserved vegetables, season to taste, and mix well. Serve immediately.

red bell peppers

INDIAN SPICED RED LENTIL AND KAMUT SOUP

Lentils are one of the healthiest pulses, providing a great source of protein and iron. This lightly spiced warming soup also benefits from the flavor of the kamut and is perfect for cold winter days.

SERVES 4-6 · PREP 20 MINS · COOK 40 MINS

1 tbsp olive oil

1 large onion, finely chopped

1 leek, trimmed and finely chopped

2in (5cm) piece of fresh ginger, finely chopped

2 tsp mild curry powder

4 carrots, unpeeled and coarsely chopped

1¼ cups red lentils

1⅔ cups uncooked kamut

1½ quarts hot vegetable stock, plus extra if needed

salt and freshly ground black pepper

1 Heat the oil in a large saucepan over medium heat. Add the onions and leeks and sauté for about 5 minutes. Then add the ginger and curry powder and stir to mix, adding a little water to the pan if they start to stick. Add the carrots, red lentils, and kamut to the pan and stir to mix.

2 Pour in 1 quart of the stock, reserving the rest. Cover, reduce the heat to a simmer, and cook for 30 minutes or until the lentils have broken down, the kamut is tender, and the carrots are cooked through. Check the soup occasionally and add more stock as needed.

3 Remove from the heat and use a handheld blender to process the soup until it reaches a chunky texture, adding more stock if necessary. Taste and season with salt and pepper. Stir well to combine and serve warm.

leeks

WINTER VEGETABLE SOUP WITH BACON AND BARLEY

This delicious combination of root vegetables, winter greens, and fluffy, wholesome barley makes a filling dish and a truly comforting meal on a cold winter day.

SERVES 4 · PREP 10 MINS · COOK 55 MINS

1 tbsp olive oil

1 onion, finely sliced

1 carrot, diced

1 parsnip, diced

1 small rutabaga, about 9oz (250g), diced

1 cup pearl barley, rinsed

6 cups vegetable stock

8 unsmoked bacon slices, cut into bite-sized pieces

1¾oz (50g) kale, coarsely chopped

salt and freshly ground black pepper

1 Heat the oil in a large saucepan over medium heat. Add the onion and cook for about 5 minutes, stirring occasionally, until softened. Then add the carrot, parsnip, and rutabaga and cook for another 5 minutes.

2 Add the barley and stock. Stir well and reduce the heat to a simmer. Cover, leaving the lid a little ajar, and cook for 30–40 minutes or until the vegetables and barley are tender.

3 Meanwhile, heat a small nonstick frying pan over medium-high heat. Add the bacon and fry for about 5 minutes or until crispy. Remove from the heat and set aside.

4 Stir the kale into the soup and cook for another 2–3 minutes or until the leaves have wilted. Remove from the heat, season to taste, and stir in the bacon. Ladle the soup into bowls and serve hot.

GRAIN EXCHANGE

For a variation, try using the same amount of any one of the following grains in place of the barley.

wheat berries

farro

spelt

why not try..

Try using the same amount of **cabbage** as the kale.

CHICKEN SOUP WITH SPELT

Using a good-quality chicken, preferably a free-range one, and making the stock from scratch will really ensure that you get the best flavor in this soup, which is boosted by the addition of the herbs.

SERVES 4-6 · PREP 20 MINS, PLUS OVERNIGHT SOAKING AND CHILLING · COOK 3 HRS

1 whole roasted chicken, about 2¼lb (1kg)

1 cup uncooked spelt, soaked overnight

1 tbsp olive oil

1 onion, finely chopped

2 garlic cloves, crushed

4 celery ribs, finely chopped

2 carrots, chopped into bite-sized pieces

2 potatoes, chopped into bite-sized pieces

½ tsp dried sage

½ tsp dried thyme

½ tsp dried rosemary

salt and freshly ground black pepper

¼ cup chopped flat-leaf parsley

FOR THE STOCK

1 onion, finely chopped

2 garlic cloves chopped

2 celery ribs, finely chopped

1 tbsp apple cider vinegar

1 Place the chicken on a clean work surface. Use two forks to coarsely shred the meat from the bones and place in a large bowl. Place the bowl in the fridge and leave to chill. Reserve the bones. Drain the spelt, rinse under running water, and drain well again. Set aside.

2 For the stock, place the bones in a large, lidded saucepan and cover with 2 quarts of water. Add the onions, garlic, celery, and vinegar. Season with ½ teaspoon of salt, cover, and simmer for at least 2 hours. Remove from the heat and skim away any fat that rises to the surface. Strain the stock into a large pan, discarding the bones and vegetables, and set aside.

3 Heat the oil in a large soup pot over medium heat. Add the onions, garlic, and celery. Cook for about 5 minutes, stirring frequently, until the onion and celery have softened. Then add the carrots, potatoes, and spelt. Stir to combine.

4 Add the strained stock to the pan, cover, and simmer for 40 minutes or until the spelt is tender. Then add the sage, thyme, rosemary, and shredded chicken. Simmer the soup for another 10 minutes or until the vegetables are cooked and the chicken has warmed through. Remove from the heat and season to taste, if needed. Garnish with parsley and serve immediately.

flat-leaf parsley

CREAMY CAULIFLOWER AND BULGUR WHEAT SOUP

A double whammy of Cheddar and Parmesan cheese really lifts this soup. The cauliflower is a classic foil for the cheese and, together with the bulgur wheat, gives the soup a lovely rich texture.

SERVES 4–6 · PREP 5 MINS · COOK 30 MINS

1 tbsp olive oil

1 onion, finely chopped

1 cauliflower, about 10oz (300g), cut into florets

1 cup uncooked bulgur wheat

1¼ quarts hot chicken stock

1 cup whole milk

1¼ cups freshly grated medium Cheddar cheese

¼ cup freshly grated Parmesan cheese

salt and freshly ground black pepper

1 Heat the oil in a large saucepan over medium heat. Add the onion and sauté for about 5 minutes or until softened. Then add the cauliflower, bulgur wheat, and stock.

2 Cover, reduce the heat to a simmer, and cook for 20–25 minutes or until the cauliflower is tender. Then remove from the heat and use a handheld blender to process the soup until smooth.

3 Return the soup to low heat. Add the milk in a slow stream, stirring constantly to combine. Then add both types of cheese, a little at a time, stirring constantly until the cheese has melted and is well combined. Remove from the heat and season to taste. Serve warm.

cauliflower

CELERY ROOT AND APPLE SOUP WITH CROUTONS

Celery root, or celeriac, is the nutritious cousin of the popular parsnip. Blending it with apple makes a perfect combination, with the fruit adding a tangy sweetness to the hearty root vegetable soup.

SERVES 4-6 · PREP 10 MINS, PLUS CHILLING · COOK 55 MINS

FOR THE CROUTONS

salt and freshly ground
    black pepper

1 cup quick-cook polenta

2 sprigs of rosemary,
    finely chopped

2 tbsp olive oil

FOR THE SOUP

2–3 tbsp olive oil

2 celery roots, tops removed,
    peeled and diced

1 white potato, diced

2 green apples, cored
    and diced

6 scallions, white parts diced
    and green parts reserved to
    garnish

salt and freshly ground
    white pepper

½ cup–1 cup freshly grated
    Gruyère cheese

1 For the croutons, place 3 cups of water in a saucepan. Add ¼ teaspoon of salt and bring to a boil. Then add the polenta, a little at a time, whisking continuously. Reduce the heat to low and cook for about 3 minutes, whisking continuously, until it has thickened. Remove from the heat.

2 Line a baking sheet with parchment paper and set aside. Season the polenta with black pepper, add the rosemary and oil, and mix to combine. Spoon the mixture into the prepared baking sheet and spread it out to form a ¼in (5mm) thick even layer. Place in the fridge and chill for 2 hours or until it firms up.

3 For the soup, heat the oil in a large, lidded saucepan over medium heat. Add the celery root, potatoes, apples, and onions. Cook for 8 minutes, stirring, until the celery root and apples are soft, but not brown. Season with salt and white pepper, add 1½ quarts of water, and bring to a boil. Reduce the heat to a simmer, cover, and cook for 30–40 minutes. Remove from the heat and process the mixture with a handheld blender, until reduced to a smooth purée. Season to taste, if needed.

4 Set the broiler at its medium setting. Remove the polenta from the sheet and cut it into four (or six) 2in (5cm) squares. Place them on a lined baking sheet, sprinkle the Gruyère cheese over them, and broil for about 3 minutes or until the cheese has melted and has started to brown. Ladle the soup into bowls and top with the croutons. Garnish with the reserved scallions and serve immediately.

THAI CURRY, TOMATO, AND VEGETABLE SOUP WITH FARRO

Tomato soup takes on a whole new life in this recipe when mixed with Thai curry paste and a variety of fresh vegetables. The addition of farro gives just the right amount of bulk to this satisfying soup.

SERVES 4 · PREP 10 MINS · COOK 1 HR 30 MINS

½ cup uncooked farro

14oz (400g) can light coconut milk

1 cup vegetable stock

6oz (175g) tomato paste

2 tbsp Thai red curry paste

1 tbsp brown sugar

1 tbsp extra virgin olive oil

2 leeks, white and light green parts only, chopped

1 green bell pepper, seeded and diced

1 zucchini, diced

1 large beefsteak tomato, diced

sea salt and freshly ground black pepper

handful of cilantro leaves, to garnish

1 Place the farro in a large, lidded saucepan and cover with water. Place over medium heat, cover, and simmer for about 1 hour or until almost all the water has been absorbed. Drain any remaining water and set aside.

2 Place a large, lidded saucepan over medium heat. Add the coconut milk, stock, tomato paste, Thai red curry paste, and brown sugar and stir to combine. Cover and bring to a boil, stirring occasionally to make sure the ingredients are well combined. Then reduce the heat to a low simmer and cook the soup for another 20 minutes.

3 Meanwhile, heat the oil in a large frying pan over medium heat. Add the leeks and green bell peppers and sauté for 10 minutes or until softened and browned in places. Add the zucchini and cook for another 3 minutes. Remove from the heat and set aside.

4 Add the tomatoes to the soup. Taste and adjust the seasoning and cook the soup, stirring once, for 5 minutes. Then add the leek mixture and the farro. Stir well to mix and remove from the heat. Ladle the soup into bowls and garnish with cilantro. Serve hot with a green salad and crusty ciabatta bread.

CHICKPEA, GARLIC, AND SPELT SOUP

This healthy and simple soup contains just the right balance of texture, from the chickpeas and spelt, and flavor, from the fresh herbs and chile flakes. Serve it with some crusty whole grain bread for a satisfying meal.

SERVES 4 · PREP 15 MINS, PLUS OVERNIGHT SOAKING · COOK 1 HR 20 MINS

¾ cup uncooked spelt

salt and freshly ground black pepper

2 tbsp extra virgin olive oil

1 onion, finely chopped

1 tsp finely chopped rosemary

1 tsp finely chopped thyme

5 garlic cloves, crushed and sliced

a pinch or two of chile flakes

14oz (400g) can chickpeas, drained

8–10 kale leaves, stalks removed and finely chopped

2 tbsp lemon juice

1¼ quarts vegetable or chicken stock

1 tbsp freshly grated Parmesan cheese, to serve

1 Place the spelt in a bowl, cover with water, and leave to soak overnight. Then drain, rinse under running water, and place in a saucepan. Cover with 3 cups of water, add a pinch of salt, and bring to a boil. Then reduce the heat to a simmer, cover, and cook for about 50 minutes, until almost all the water has been absorbed. Remove from the heat and drain any remaining water. Cover and set aside.

2 Heat the oil in a large, heavy-bottomed pot over medium heat. Add the onions and cook for 2–3 minutes, stirring frequently, until softened. Then add the rosemary, thyme, garlic, and chile flakes. Season with ½ teaspoon of salt and a good grinding of pepper. Cook, stirring, for about 2 minutes.

3 Add the chickpeas, kale, and lemon juice to the pot. Stir to combine and cook until the kale has just started to wilt. Add the stock and bring to a boil. Then reduce the heat to a simmer and cook for about 15 minutes. Add the spelt and cook for another 5 minutes, stirring frequently. Remove from the heat, sprinkle with Parmesan, and serve warm.

thyme

LIGHT ASIAN COCONUT BROTH WITH CHICKEN AND MILLET

This light soup contains many ingredients that are popular in Asian cuisine. It is given an extra boost by the use of coconut oil, which contains nutrients to protect the heart and improve the immune system.

SERVES 2 · PREP 10 MINS · COOK 40 MINS

2 tbsp coconut oil

2 chicken thighs, cut into cubes

2in (5cm) piece of fresh ginger, finely chopped

1 garlic clove, finely chopped

½ red chile, seeded and finely chopped

1 cup coconut milk

2 cups chicken stock

1½ cup uncooked millet

7oz (200g) bean sprouts

1 tbsp soy sauce

2 tbsp chopped cilantro leaves, to garnish

1 Heat the oil in a large saucepan over medium-high heat. Add the chicken to the pan and cook for about 5 minutes, stirring frequently, until evenly colored all over.

2 Add the ginger, garlic, and chile and cook for 2 minutes, stirring frequently. Then stir in the coconut milk, stock, and millet. Reduce the heat to a simmer and cook for about 15–20 minutes.

3 Add the bean sprouts to the pan and cook for 10 minutes, until the millet is fluffy and the chicken has cooked through. Then stir in the soy sauce. Divide the broth equally between two soup bowls and garnish with the cilantro. Serve hot.

cilantro

WARM
AND COOL
SALADS

NUTTY BARLEY AND LENTiL SALAD

This is no boring salad! The combination of hearty barley and nutty, crunchy almonds and walnuts is well balanced by the contrasting tastes and textures of sweet, dried cranberries and salty goat cheese.

SERVES 4 · PREP 10 MiNS, PLUS OVERNiGHT SOAKiNG AND COOLiNG · COOK 30 MiNS

⅓ cup uncooked pearl barley

14oz (400g) can green lentils, drained

¼ cup almonds, coarsely chopped

¼ cup walnuts, coarsely chopped

⅓ cup dried cranberries

⅓ cup soft goat cheese, crumbled

3½oz (100g) arugula

1 Place the barley in a bowl, cover with water, and leave to soak overnight or for at least 8 hours. Then drain, rinse under running water, and drain well again.

2 Place the barley in a lidded saucepan and cover with plenty of water. Bring to a boil, then reduce the heat to a simmer, and cover. Cook for about 30 minutes or until the barley is tender. Remove from the heat, drain any remaining water, and leave to cool completely.

3 Once cooled, place the barley and lentils in a large bowl and mix lightly to combine. Add the almonds, walnuts, and cranberries and mix to combine. Sprinkle in the goat cheese, add the arugula, and toss lightly. Divide the salad equally between four plates and serve immediately.

GRAiN EXCHANGE
Use the same amount of **wheat berries** in place of the barley and see p16–17 for advice on cooking times.

why not try..

You could try the same amount of **sunflower seeds** or chopped **Brazil nuts** instead of the almonds or walnuts. You could also replace the arugula with the same quantity of **flat-leaf parsley**.

RAINBOW WHEAT BERRY AND FETA CHEESE SALAD

This healthy salad is bursting with flavors and textures that bring together the nuttiness of the chewy wheat berries, the rich and soft feta, and the sweet and crunchy pomegranate seeds.

SERVES 2 · PREP 20 MINS, PLUS OVERNIGHT SOAKING AND COOLING · COOK 30 MINS

¼ cup uncooked wheat berries

1 carrot, grated

1 zucchini, grated

⅓ cup pumpkin seeds

⅔ cup feta cheese, crumbled

2 tbsp chopped flat-leaf parsley

seeds of 1 small pomegranate

salt and freshly ground black pepper

juice of 1 lemon (optional)

1 Place the wheat berries in a bowl, cover with water, and leave to soak overnight or for at least 8 hours. Then drain, rinse under running water, and drain well again.

2 Place the wheat berries in a lidded saucepan, cover with plenty of water, and bring to a boil, then reduce the heat to a simmer, and cover. Cook for 30 minutes, until the wheat berries are tender. Remove from the heat, drain any remaining water, and leave to cool completely.

3 Once cooled, place the wheat berries, carrots, and zucchini in a large bowl. Sprinkle in the pumpkin seeds and mix lightly to combine. Add the feta and parsley to the mixture and toss to combine.

4 Divide the salad equally between two salad bowls or plates. Sprinkle over the pomegranate seeds and season to taste. Drizzle with lemon juice, if using, and serve immediately.

GRAiN EXCHANGE

You could replace the wheat berries with the same quantity of one of the following grains.

farro

spelt

barley

why not try...

In place of the carrot, try adding a **finely chopped red bell pepper.** You could replace the zucchini with a quarter of **finely shredded red cabbage**.

MEDITERRANEAN TUNA AND FARRO SALAD

Farro makes a great substitute for rice and, with a traditional southern European medley of tomatoes, olives, and red onions, this lovely light salad is a great reminder of warm summer vacations.

SERVES 4 · PREP 15 MINS · COOK 30 MINS

½ cup uncooked farro

2 x 5oz (142g) can tuna in spring water or brine, drained

5 sun-dried tomatoes in oil, coarsely chopped

2½oz (70g) green olives, pitted and halved

1 small red onion, diced

1 small red bell pepper, seeded and cut into bite-sized pieces

1 small zucchini, cut into bite-sized pieces

3½oz (100g) mixed salad leaves

¼ cup chopped basil, to garnish

FOR THE DRESSING

3 tbsp extra virgin olive oil

2 tbsp balsamic vinegar

½ tsp Italian seasoning

1 garlic clove, crushed

salt and freshly ground black pepper

1 Place the farro in a large saucepan and cover with water. Bring to a boil, and then reduce the heat to a simmer. Cook for about 30 minutes or until tender. Remove from the heat, drain any remaining water, and leave to cool.

2 Use a fork to roughly flake the tuna from the cans and place in a large bowl. Add the tomatoes, olives, onions, red pepper, and zucchini and mix well. Then add the cooled farro and mix until well combined.

3 For the dressing, place all the ingredients in a bowl and mix to combine. Taste and season with salt and pepper, if needed. Place the salad leaves on serving plates. Top with the tuna and farro mixture and pour in the dressing. Toss lightly to coat and garnish with basil. Serve immediately.

zucchini

CHICKEN AND PEANUT KAMUT SALAD

This nutty salad is a great way to use leftover chicken with a hint of lime for a zesty finish.

SERVES 2 · PREP 10 MINS, PLUS SOAKING · COOK 45 MINS

¾ cup uncooked kamut	2 tbsp salted peanuts
10oz (300g) cooked chicken breasts or thighs, shredded	2 tbsp chopped cilantro leaves, to garnish
4 scallions, finely chopped	**FOR THE DRESSING**
	2 tbsp smooth peanut butter
salt and freshly ground black pepper	juice of 1 lime

1 Place the kamut in a large bowl and cover with water. Leave to soak for 8 hours or for up to 24 hours. Then drain, rinse under running water, and drain well again.

2 Place the kamut in a large saucepan, cover with water, and bring to a boil. Then reduce the heat to a simmer and cook for 40–45 minutes. Remove from the heat and drain any remaining water. Set aside and keep warm.

3 For the dressing, place the peanut butter and lime juice in a small bowl. Add 2 tablespoons of water and whisk until well combined and thickened to the consistency of heavy cream.

4 Place the warm kamut in a large bowl. Add the chicken and onions and toss lightly to mix. Then pour the dressing in, season to taste, and mix well. Sprinkle the peanuts over the top, garnish with cilantro, and serve immediately.

WARM HARISSA, SORGHUM, AND CHICKPEA SALAD

Harissa spices are combined with light and chewy sorghum for a Middle Eastern-inspired salad.

SERVES 4 · PREP 5 MINS · COOK 1 HR

1 cup uncooked sorghum	1 tbsp harissa paste
2 red bell peppers, seeded and cut into bite-sized pieces	juice of 1 lemon
	salt and freshly ground black pepper
2 red onions, diced	3½oz (100g) arugula leaves
1 tbsp olive oil	
2 x 14oz (400g) can chickpeas, drained	¼ cup chopped flat-leaf parsley, to garnish

1 Rinse the sorghum under running water and place in a large, lidded saucepan. Cover with water and bring to a boil. Then reduce the heat to a simmer and cook, covered, for 50–60 minutes, until tender. Remove from the heat, drain any remaining water, and transfer to a large bowl.

2 Meanwhile, preheat the oven to 400°F (200°C). Place the red bell peppers and onions in a baking sheet. Drizzle the oil over them and toss to coat. Bake in the oven for 30–40 minutes, until softened. Remove from the heat. Add the red bell peppers and onions to the sorghum and mix well.

3 Add the chickpeas and harissa paste to the sorghum mixture. Toss to combine, making sure the vegetables and chickpeas are evenly covered with the paste. Pour in the lemon juice and season to taste. Divide the arugula between four plates and top with the sorghum salad. Garnish with parsley and serve immediately.

MEXICAN QUINOA SALAD

Fresh vegetables, crunchy tortilla chips, and spicy chiles come together to create a dish that packs a real punch in flavor and texture. A salad that everyone can enjoy.

SERVES 2 · PREP 15 MINS, PLUS COOLING · COOK 20 MINS

⅓ cup uncooked quinoa

14oz (400g) can red kidney beans, drained

¼ cup canned corn

½ red onion, finely chopped

1 red bell pepper, seeded and finely chopped

4–6 slices pickled jalapeño chiles, finely chopped

1 avocado, pitted and cut into cubes

1 head of romaine lettuce

1¾oz (50g) plain corn tortilla chips, crumbled, plus extra to serve

1 lemon or lime, halved, to serve

1 Rinse the quinoa under running water, drain, and place in a lidded saucepan. Cover with 1 cup of water and bring to a boil.

2 Reduce the heat to a simmer, cover, and cook for 15–20 minutes or until almost all the liquid has been absorbed and the quinoa is fluffy. Remove from the heat, drain any remaining water, and set aside to cool.

3 Place the quinoa, kidney beans, corn, onions, peppers, and jalapeños in a large bowl. Mix until well combined. Then add the avocado and mix lightly to combine.

4 Roughly shred the lettuce and add to the bowl. Sprinkle the tortillas over the mixture and toss lightly. Transfer the salad to a serving platter or plate. Serve immediately with tortilla chips and lemons or limes to squeeze over the dish.

GRAIN EXCHANGE

Instead of the quinoa, use the same quantity of **millet**.

why not try...

Use a 14oz (400g) can of **black beans**, drained, in place of the kidney beans.

AVOCADO, CiLANTRO, AND LiME TABBOULEH

Tabbouleh is traditionally served as part of a mezze in the Middle East, but it also makes an excellent salad on its own or to accompany cold meats. The lime and avocado in this version give it a really fresh dimension.

SERVES 4 · PREP 15 MiNS, PLUS SOAKiNG AND CHiLLiNG

1⅓ cups bulgur wheat

1½ tsp rock salt

2 tomatoes, diced

1 avocado, peeled, pitted, and diced

1 small red bell pepper, seeded and diced

⅓ cup red onion, diced

handful of cilantro leaves, roughly chopped

½ cup lime juice

2 tbsp extra virgin olive oil

salt and freshly ground black pepper

1 Place 1½ cups of water in a large saucepan and bring to a boil. Place the bulgur wheat and rock salt in a large bowl. Pour the boiling water in the bowl, cover, and leave to soak for about 30 minutes.

2 Drain any excess water from the bulgur wheat and place it in a large bowl. Then add the tomatoes, avocado, red bell peppers, onions, and cilantro. Mix well to combine. Transfer the mixture to a large serving bowl.

3 Drizzle the lime juice and oil over the mixture. Toss well to coat. Season to taste with salt and black pepper, if needed. Mix well and chill the tabbouleh in the fridge for about 20 minutes before serving.

TOMATO, GOAT CHEESE, AND WATERMELON STACKS WITH TOASTED SPELT

The perfect healthy salad for a warm summer day, the contrasting textures and flavors, from the toasted spelt, creamy goat cheese, and refreshing watermelon, make an excellent combination.

MAKES 4 STACKS · PREP 20 MINS, PLUS OVERNIGHT SOAKING · COOK 50 MINS

¾ cup uncooked spelt, soaked

salt and freshly ground black pepper

1 tbsp olive oil

2 beefsteak tomatoes, about 1¼lb (550g) in total, sliced into 8 rounds

¾ cup goat cheese, sliced into thin rounds

3lb 3oz (1½kg) watermelon, seeded and sliced into rounds

handful of basil leaves

a good drizzle of extra virgin olive oil

1 Place the spelt in a large bowl, cover with water, and leave to soak overnight or for about 8 hours. Then drain, rinse under running water, and drain well again.

2 Place the spelt in a lidded saucepan. Cover with 3 cups of water, add a pinch of salt, and bring to a boil. Then reduce the heat to a simmer and cover. Cook for about 40 minutes, until all the water has been absorbed. Remove from the heat and drain the remaining water. Heat the olive oil in a large nonstick frying pan over medium heat. Add the spelt and cook for about 10 minutes, stirring frequently, until golden brown. Remove from the heat and leave to cool.

3 To assemble the stacks, place a slice of tomato on each of four serving plates and season with salt and pepper. Top each one with a slice of cheese, a slice of watermelon, and a few basil leaves. Repeat to get one more layer of each, then sprinkle a few spoonfuls of the toasted spelt on top. Drizzle over the extra virgin olive oil and season to taste if needed. Serve immediately.

watermelon

MEDITERRANEAN SALAD BOATS

The flavors of the Mediterranean come together in this quick and easy salad that is as colorful as it is satisfying.

SERVES 4 · PREP 15 MINS

1 large tomato, seeded and diced

1 cucumber, diced

1 red bell pepper, seeded and diced

2½oz (70g) kalamata olives, pitted and halved

¾ cup feta cheese, crumbled

1 cup prepared quinoa (see p22)

2 tbsp extra virgin olive oil

2 tbsp lemon juice

1 garlic clove, crushed

1 tbsp chopped oregano

salt and freshly ground black pepper

1 romaine heart, leaves separated

1 Place the tomatoes, cucumber, red bell pepper, olives, feta, and quinoa in a large bowl and toss to combine. Place the oil, lemon juice, garlic, and oregano in a separate bowl. Whisk to combine.

2 Pour the oil mixture over the salad and toss to coat. Season to taste with salt and pepper and divide the salad between four serving plates. Top with equal quantities of the romaine leaves and serve immediately.

STRAWBERRY, FETA, AND WHEAT BERRY SALAD

Sweet strawberries pair perfectly with wheat berries and salty feta cheese in this cooling and fruity salad.

SERVES 2 · PREP 10 MINS, PLUS OVERNIGHT SOAKING AND COOLING · COOK 30 MINS

½ cup uncooked wheat berries

1 tbsp balsamic vinegar

3 tbsp extra virgin olive oil

salt and freshly ground black pepper

1½oz (40g) baby spinach

3½oz (100g) strawberries, trimmed and cut into bite-sized pieces

½ cup basil leaves, finely chopped

½ cup feta cheese, crumbled

1 Place the wheat berries in a large bowl and cover with water. Leave to soak overnight or for about 8 hours. Then drain, rinse under running water, and drain well again.

2 Place the wheat berries in a large, lidded saucepan, cover with water, and bring to a boil. Then reduce the heat to a simmer, cover, and cook for about 30 minutes or until tender but chewy. Remove from the heat and discard any remaining water. Transfer to a large bowl and leave to cool for at least 10 minutes.

3 Meanwhile, place the balsamic vinegar and oil in a small bowl and mix until well combined. Season to taste and mix well. Add the spinach, strawberries, and basil to the wheat berries and mix well. Then add the feta and pour in the dressing. Toss to coat, making sure the feta is evenly distributed. Serve immediately.

WARM ROASTED BUTTERNUT SQUASH AND WHEAT BERRY SALAD

A great dish for cool, fall days, this tangy salad is an excellent combination of sweet, roasted butternut squash and chewy wheat berries that are given an added salty element from the blue cheese.

SERVES 4 · PREP 15 MINS, PLUS OVERNIGHT SOAKING AND COOLING · COOK 1 HR

1¾ cups uncooked
wheat berries

1¾lb (800g) butternut
squash, seeded and
cut into cubes

2 tbsp olive oil, plus extra
for greasing

salt and freshly ground
black pepper

1 cup blue cheese, such as
Danish Blue, crumbled

½ cup balsamic vinegar

1 Place the wheat berries in a large bowl, cover with water, and leave to soak overnight or for about 8 hours. Then drain, rinse under running water, and drain well again.

2 Place the wheat berries in a large, lidded saucepan and cover with 1 quart of water. Bring to a boil, and then reduce the heat to medium-low, cover, and simmer for about 50 minutes. Remove from the heat, drain any remaining water, and leave to cool slightly.

3 Meanwhile, preheat the oven to 400°F (200°C). Grease a baking sheet with a little oil. Spread out the butternut squash on the sheet in an even layer and drizzle the oil over them. Season to taste and roast in the oven for 20 minutes. Then remove from the heat, stir to mix, and return to the oven. Roast for another 20 minutes.

4 Place the wheat berries, butternut squash, and cheese in a large bowl and toss to combine. Drizzle the balsamic vinegar in the bowl and toss to coat. Taste and adjust the seasoning, if needed, and serve immediately.

butternut squash

GRiLLED BROCCOLi RABE AND BARLEY
WiTH A ROMESCO SAUCE

A tasty vegetarian recipe, this dish can be served as a filling main meal or even an impressive side. The flavor of the broccoli is enhanced by grilling and is well paired with the spicy Spanish sauce and fluffy barley.

SERVES 6-8 · PREP 10 MiNS, PLUS SOAKING · COOK 1 HR 5 MiNS

1 cup uncooked barley

salt and freshly ground
  black pepper

1lb 5oz (600g) broccoli rabe

2 tbsp extra virgin olive oil

juice of ½ lemon

FOR THE SAUCE

⅔ cup dried ancho chiles,
  seeded

½ cup almonds, sliced

3½oz (100g) roasted red
  peppers from a jar

14oz (400g) can chopped
  tomatoes

2 tbsp sherry vinegar

2 tbsp extra virgin olive oil

pinch of smoked paprika

1 Place the barley in a large saucepan and cover with 3 cups of water. Add a pinch of salt and bring to a boil. Then reduce the heat to a simmer, cover, and cook for about 50 minutes or until almost all the water has been absorbed. Remove from the heat. Cover and set aside.

2 Meanwhile, for the sauce, place the ancho chiles in a small bowl, cover with water, and leave to soak for 10 minutes. Then drain the chiles and discard the water. Dice the chiles and set them aside. Place the almonds in a nonstick frying pan over medium-low heat. Toast the almonds for 3–4 minutes or until lightly browned. Transfer the almonds to a food processor and pulse until they form a coarse flour.

3 Add the ancho chiles, roasted red peppers, tomatoes, sherry vinegar, oil, and smoked paprika to the food processor. Season with ¼ teaspoon of salt and a good grinding of pepper. Pulse until the mixture is smooth, but retains a little texture. Transfer the sauce to a bowl and set aside.

4 Place the broccoli in a large bowl. Drizzle the oil in, season to taste, and toss to coat. Heat a griddle pan over medium-high heat. Grill the broccoli for 3–5 minutes on each side, until tender and starting to brown.

5 Remove the broccoli from the heat and drizzle in the lemon juice. On a large serving dish, spread out the barley and top with the broccoli. Pour over the desired quantity of romesco sauce. Serve immediately with the remaining sauce on the side.

CAPRESE FARRO SALAD

Featuring fresh summer tomatoes, soft mozzarella, chewy farro, and a homemade pesto sauce, this colorful and light italian salad makes the perfect starter for any meal.

SERVES 4 · PREP 10 MINS, PLUS COOLING · COOK 50 MINS

1 cup uncooked farro

8oz (225g) mozzarella, diced

3 large tomatoes, cut into bite-sized pieces

FOR THE PESTO

1 cup basil leaves, rinsed and dried, plus extra to garnish

2 tbsp pine nuts

1 garlic clove

2–3 tbsp extra virgin olive oil

salt

1 Rinse the farro under cold running water and place in a large saucepan. Cover with about 2½ cups of water and bring to a boil. Then reduce the heat to a simmer and cook, stirring occasionally, for about 40 minutes or until softened. Remove from the heat, drain, and set aside to cool.

2 For the pesto, place the basil leaves, pine nuts, garlic, and oil in a food processor and pulse until smooth. Season to taste, if needed.

3 Place the mozzarella and tomatoes in a large bowl. Add the pesto and cooled farro and stir to mix. Chill the salad in the fridge until ready to serve, garnished with a few basil leaves.

GRAIN EXCHANGE

For a change, try using the same amount of **pearl barley** in place of the farro.

why not try...

You could replace the fresh mozzarella cheese with the same quantity of **burrata** cheese.

MiLLET, CORN, AND RED PEPPER SALAD
WiTH ROASTED LEEKS

Serving this light and healthy salad over leeks gives it a wonderful twist. The addition of yogurt provides the dish with a rich and creamy texture that is well balanced with the crunchiness of the peppers.

SERVES 6 · PREP 15 MiNS · COOK 40 MiNS

4 tbsp olive oil

½ cup uncooked millet

salt and freshly ground black pepper

1 small red onion, diced

2 red bell peppers, seeded and diced

1 jalapeño, diced

½ tbsp cayenne pepper

4 whole ears of corn, kernels removed

2 large poblano chiles, roasted, peeled, seeded, and sliced into small strips

½ tsp smoked paprika

3 scallions, thinly sliced

½ cup plain yogurt

juice of 1 lime

6 leeks, bottoms and rough green tops trimmed, cleaned, and halved lengthwise

1 Heat 1 tablespoon of the oil in a large, lidded saucepan over medium heat. Add the millet and cook for 2–3 minutes, stirring frequently. Add ¼ teaspoon of salt, cover with 2 cups of water, and bring to a boil. Reduce the heat to a simmer, cover, and cook for 15 minutes. Remove from the heat. Leave to soak, covered, for about 10 minutes, then use a fork to fluff up the grain. Leave to cool.

2 Meanwhile, heat 1 tablespoon of the oil in a frying pan over medium heat. Add the onions and red bell peppers and season well. Cook for 5 minutes, stirring, until the onions are translucent. Then add the jalapeños, cayenne pepper, corn, chiles, and smoked paprika. Cook for another 5–10 minutes, stirring occasionally, until the corn is tender.

3 Reduce the heat to low and add the scallions and yogurt. Cook for about 2 minutes, stirring, until the yogurt has melted. Then add the lime juice and season to taste. Transfer the mixture to a large bowl, add the cooled millet, and mix to combine. Set aside.

4 Set the broiler at its medium setting. Brush the leeks with the remaining oil and season well. Broil the leeks for 20 minutes, turning over frequently, until tender and cooked through. Then transfer to a plate, cover with foil, and leave to steam for 5 minutes. Place the leeks on serving plates and spoon the corn and millet salad over them. Serve warm.

CHiCKEN CAESAR SALAD WiTH POLENTA CROUTONS

This perennially popular salad is given a twist with the use of baked polenta to make crunchy croutons that provide extra texture to complement the succulence of the chicken and the freshness of the lettuce.

SERVES 4 · PREP 20 MiNS · COOK 10 MiNS

2 tbsp olive oil

1 cup prepared polenta (see p25), cut into 1in (2.5cm) cubes

½ tsp rock salt

¼ tsp freshly ground black pepper

1 large or 2 small heads romaine lettuce, washed, dried, and torn into bite-sized pieces

8oz (225g) cooked chicken, cut into bite-sized pieces

¾ cup freshly grated Romano cheese

FOR THE DRESSiNG

½ cup extra virgin olive oil

1 tbsp Dijon mustard

3 tbsp good-quality mayonnaise

4 anchovy fillets, chopped

½ tsp Worcestershire sauce

1 garlic clove, crushed

2 tbsp finely grated Parmesan cheese, plus extra to serve

pinch of sugar

1 Heat the oil in a large frying pan over medium heat. Add the polenta and season with ½ teaspoon of salt and ¼ teaspoon of pepper. Cook for 10 minutes, turning over the polenta cubes occasionally, until crisp and lightly browned. Remove from the heat and set aside.

2 For the dressing, place all the ingredients in the small bowl of a food processor and pulse until emulsified into a thick and creamy dressing. Alternatively, place the ingredients in a large bowl and blend well with a handheld blender. Season with pepper, mix well to combine, and set aside.

3 Place the lettuce, chicken, and cheese in a large bowl and toss lightly to combine. Drizzle over the dressing, a little at a time, and toss until well coated. Arrange the salad on a serving dish and scatter the polenta croutons over it. Sprinkle over some Parmesan and serve immediately.

CARAMELIZED ONION AND KALE WHEAT BERRY SALAD WITH GRILLED STEAK

A great meal to enjoy al fresco, sweet caramelized onions and earthy kale are combined with nutty wheat berries in this crunchy summer salad. If preferred, you can use a different cut of steak, such as rump or fillet.

SERVES 4 · PREP 10 MINS, PLUS OVERNIGHT SOAKING AND RESTING · COOK 1 HR 20 MINS

1½ cups wheat berries, soaked overnight

1lb (450g) sirloin steak

salt and freshly ground black pepper

2 tbsp olive oil

2 onions, halved and thinly sliced

3½oz (100g) kale, coarsely chopped

1½ cups balsamic vinegar

1 Place the wheat berries in a lidded saucepan and cover with 1 quart of water. Bring to a boil, then reduce the heat to medium-low, and cover. Cook for about 50 minutes or until all the water has been absorbed. Remove from the heat, drain any remaining water, and place in a large bowl. Set aside.

2 Set the broiler at its medium setting and season the steak on both sides. Broil the steak for 6–8 minutes, on each side, or until cooked to the desired doneness. Remove from the heat and leave to rest and cool for at least 10 minutes. Then slice the steak into thin strips and set aside.

3 Heat the oil in a large frying pan over medium heat. Add the onions and season well. Cook, stirring frequently, for 10–15 minutes, until softened and golden brown. Then add the kale and vinegar, cover, and cook for about 5 minutes or until the kale has softened slightly. Remove from the heat.

5 Add the onion and kale mixture to the wheat berries and toss well to combine. Divide the salad evenly among four plates and top with the sliced steak. Serve immediately.

kale

CHOPPED KALE, FREEKEH, ZUCCHINI, AND CORN SALAD
WITH GARLIC TAHINI

Chopped salads are easy to throw together and a great way to use up surplus ingredients in the fridge. Beautifully summery, this salad is best served when zucchini and corn are in their peak season.

SERVES 4–6 · PREP 20 MINS, PLUS COOLING · COOK 30 MINS

1 cup uncooked freekeh

2½ cups vegetable stock

2 ears of corn

1 tbsp olive oil

¾ cup almonds, coarsely chopped

¼ cup sesame seeds

10–12 kale leaves, ribs removed and finely chopped

14oz (400g) can chickpeas

4–6 scallions, chopped

1 green zucchini, diced

1 yellow zucchini, diced

FOR THE DRESSING

3 tbsp tahini

1 garlic clove, pressed

2 tbsp lemon juice

1 tsp low-sodium soy sauce

1 tsp toasted sesame oil

salt and freshly ground black pepper

1 Rinse the freekeh under cold running water, drain well, and place in a lidded saucepan. Add the stock and bring to a boil. Then reduce the heat to a simmer, cover, and cook for about 20 minutes. Remove from the heat and leave to stand, covered, for 5 minutes. Then uncover and leave to cool completely.

2 Bring a large pan of water to a boil. Add the corn and cook for 10 minutes or until the corn kernels are tender. Remove from the pan and rinse under cold running water. Remove the kernels from the cob by slicing down lengthwise with a knife.

3 For the dressing, place the tahini, garlic, lemon juice, soy sauce, and sesame oil in a small bowl. Add 2 tablespoons of water and whisk until well combined. Taste and adjust the seasoning, if necessary, and set aside.

4 Heat the olive oil in a small nonstick frying pan over low heat. Add the almonds and sesame seeds and toast for 2–3 minutes or until the almonds are lightly browned. Remove from the heat and leave to cool.

5 Place the kale in a large bowl and drizzle with some of the dressing. Toss well to coat. Then add the corn, almonds, sesame seeds, chickpeas, scallions, and green and yellow zucchini. Drizzle over more of the seasoning and toss well to coat. Add the freekeh and the remaining seasoning and mix well to combine. Serve immediately.

QUINOA AND FENNEL SALAD

The peppery and licorice notes of fennel are combined with the scallions and cilantro in this salad and contrast well with the nuttiness of the quinoa and the juicy and sweet pomegranate seeds.

SERVES 4 · PREP 10 MINS, PLUS STANDING · COOK 15 MINS

1 cup uncooked quinoa

1½ cups vegetable stock

1 tsp ground cumin

1 whole fennel bulb

3 tbsp olive oil

1 tbsp lemon juice

salt and freshly ground black pepper

4 scallions, trimmed and thinly sliced

3 tbsp chopped cilantro leaves

2 tbsp chopped mint leaves

3½oz (100g) pomegranate seeds

1 Rinse the quinoa under cold running water. Drain and place in a large saucepan. Add the stock and cumin and bring to a boil, stirring frequently. Then cover and cook over medium heat for about 10 minutes. Remove from the heat and drain. Return the quinoa to the pan and leave for about 10 minutes, covered, to fluff up.

2 To prepare the fennel, trim the stalks, root end, and any tough outer pieces from the bulb and reserve the fronds. Cut the bulb in half lengthwise. Then set each half on a cutting board, flat-side down, and cut into thin slices lengthwise.

3 Heat 2 tablespoons of the oil in a large frying pan over medium heat. Add the fennel slices and cook for about 5 minutes, turning over once, until golden. Remove from the heat and transfer to a bowl. Add the lemon juice and remaining oil, season to taste, and mix well to combine.

4 Add the onions, cilantro, mint, and reserved fennel fronds to the bowl. Then add the quinoa and half the pomegranate seeds. Stir to mix; taste and adjust the seasoning, if needed. Divide the salad between four plates and sprinkle the remaining pomegranate seeds over it. Serve at room temperature or cold.

FREEKEH SWEET AND SPICY WARM SALAD

This warming and colorful salad combines sweet roasted squash and sticky dates with a fragrant and spiced freekeh and is perfect for fall and winter lunches.

SERVES 4 · PREP 15 MINS, PLUS COOLING · COOK 40 MINS

2 tsp ground cinnamon

1 tsp grated ginger

1 tsp ground cumin

2 tbsp olive oil

1 butternut squash, seeded and cut into ¾in (2cm) cubes

1 cup cracked freekeh

1 small head radicchio, coarsely chopped

8 dried pitted dates, about 1½oz (40g) in total, coarsely chopped

¼ cup coarsely chopped flat-leaf parsley

FOR THE DRESSING

¼ cup extra virgin olive oil

juice of 1 lemon

1 tbsp honey

salt and freshly ground black pepper

1 Preheat the oven to 400°F (200°C). Place the cinnamon, ginger, cumin, and oil in a small bowl and mix to combine. Place the butternut squash in a rimmed baking sheet, pour the mixture over the squash, and toss to coat. Bake in the oven for 30–35 minutes or until the squash is tender.

2 Meanwhile, rinse the freekeh under running water and place in a large saucepan. Cover with 1 quart of water and bring to a boil. Then reduce the heat to a simmer and cook for 15 minutes or until almost all the water has been absorbed. Remove from the heat, drain any remaining water, and leave to cool slightly.

3 For the dressing, place all the ingredients in a bowl. Season to taste and mix to combine. Place the radicchio and dates in a large serving dish. Add the squash and freekeh and toss lightly to mix. Then pour in the dressing, season to taste, and toss until well combined. Serve warm garnished with parsley.

GRAIN EXCHANGE

This dish works well with a variety of similar grains. Try replacing the freekeh with the same amount of the following grains.

quinoa

farro

millet

why not try...

Try using 2 large **sweet potatoes** in place of the squash, and cook in the same way. You can also use **chicory** or **arugula leaves** instead of the radicchio.

SAVORY STIR-FRIES

CHINESE 5-SPICE PORK WITH MILLET

This easy-to-make stir-fry brings together tender pork, light and fresh greens, and chewy millet. Sweet and spicy, it's perfect for a quick yet flavor-packed lunch or dinner.

SERVES 4 · PREP 10 MINS, PLUS MARINATING · COOK 40 MINS

¼ cup honey

6 tbsp soy sauce

2 tbsp Chinese 5-spice powder

1lb (450g) pork tenderloin, cut into bite-sized pieces

1 cup uncooked millet

2 tbsp olive oil

10oz (300g) spring greens, cores removed and cut into ribbons

7oz (200g) bok choy, cores removed and cut into ribbons

1 Place the honey, soy sauce, and 5-spice powder in a bowl and mix to combine. Add the pork and mix until well coated. Cover the bowl with plastic wrap and place in the fridge. Leave to marinate for at least 2 hours or up to 24 hours.

2 Place the millet and ½ cup water in a large saucepan and bring to a boil. Then reduce the heat to a simmer and cook for about 15 minutes or until all the water has been absorbed and the millet is cooked through. Remove from the heat and set aside.

3 Heat the oil in a large saucepan over medium-high heat. Add the pork and marinade to the pan and cook, stirring occasionally, for about 10 minutes or until the pork is cooked through. Do this in batches to avoid overcrowding the pan. Remove with a slotted spoon and set aside.

4 Increase the heat to high and add ¼ cup of water to the pan. Stir to mix with any marinade left in the pan and bring to a boil. Then add the spring greens and bok choy and cook for 3–4 minutes until tender. Return the pork to the pan and stir in the millet. Stir well to combine and remove from the heat. Serve hot.

GRAIN EXCHANGE

Try using one of the following grains in place of the millet. For the quinoa, you can use the same amount of grain as the millet and cook as given in the recipe. For the kamut, use ¾ cup of grain and see p16–17 for advice on cooking times.

quinoa

kamut

why not try...

In place of spring greens, try adding the same amount of **broccoli** or **kale**.

THAI PEANUT AND WHEAT BERRY STIR-FRY

Peanut butter works well with rich soy beans and wheat berries to create a light, yet filling, stir-fry.

SERVES 2 · PREP 10 MINS, PLUS OVERNIGHT SOAKING
COOK 1 HR

½ cup uncooked wheat berries	1¾oz (50g) green cabbage, shredded
2 tbsp smooth peanut butter	1 carrot, sliced into matchsticks
2 tbsp honey	3½oz (100g) soy beans
1 tbsp soy sauce	salt and freshly ground black pepper
¼ tsp chile flakes	2 tbsp coarsely chopped cilantro leaves, to garnish
juice of 1 lime	
1 tbsp vegetable oil	
2½oz (75g) bean sprouts	

1 Place the wheat berries in a bowl and cover with water. Leave to soak for 8 hours or up to 24 hours. Then drain, rinse under running water, and drain again. Place in a pan, cover with water, and bring to a boil. Then reduce the heat to a simmer, cover, and cook for 40–45 minutes, until tender. Remove from the heat and drain any remaining water.

2 Place the peanut butter, honey, soy sauce, and chile flakes in a bowl and mix to combine. Then add the lime juice and mix until it forms a smooth sauce. Heat the oil in a large frying pan over high heat. Add the bean sprouts, cabbage, and carrots and stir-fry for 3–5 minutes. Then add the soy beans and wheat berries and stir-fry for another 2 minutes. Pour in the peanut sauce and toss to coat. Season to taste and remove from the heat. Sprinkle with cilantro and serve hot.

GARLIC AND GINGER BEEF WITH GREENS AND SPELT

Spring greens make a tasty alternative to bok choy in this classic beef and ginger combination.

SERVES 2 · PREP 15 MINS, PLUS OVERNIGHT SOAKING
COOK 45 MINS

½ cup uncooked spelt, soaked overnight	1 tbsp honey
2 tbsp olive oil	1 tbsp soy sauce, plus extra if needed
2in (5cm) piece of fresh ginger, grated	3½oz (100g) spring greens, shredded
3 garlic cloves, crushed	
10oz (300g) flat-iron steak, cut into strips	

1 Rinse the spelt under running water, drain well, and place in a large, lidded saucepan. Cover with water and bring to a boil. Then reduce the heat to a simmer, cover, and cook for 40 minutes.

2 Heat the oil in a large frying pan over medium heat. Add the ginger and garlic and sauté for about 5 minutes. Increase the heat to medium-high, add the beef, and cook for 3 minutes. Then add the honey and soy sauce, mix well, and increase the heat to high. Cook, stirring frequently, for 2 minutes or until the liquid is reduced to a thick sauce.

3 Reduce the heat to medium. Add the spring greens and toss lightly to combine. Then add the spelt and mix well. Cook for 3–4 minutes, stirring, until the spring greens are lightly cooked. Taste, and add more soy sauce if needed. Remove from the heat and serve hot.

EGGPLANT, ZUCCHINI, KALE, AND BUCKWHEAT STIR-FRY
WITH A GINGER MISO

This delicious and colorful dish includes a variety of vegetables, as well as hearty and filling buckwheat, and can be served as an appetizer or even a main meal. Try to use the traditional Japanese eggplants because they are sweeter than regular ones.

SERVES 4 · PREP 15 MINS · COOK 15 MINS

sea salt

1 cup uncooked buckwheat

3 tbsp canola oil

2 dried red chiles

1 garlic clove, thinly sliced

1 tsp grated fresh ginger

drizzle of toasted sesame oil (optional)

4 Japanese eggplants, cut into cubes

2 zucchini, cut into cubes

4 kale leaves, ribs removed and coarsely chopped

handful of basil leaves, coarsely chopped

sesame seeds, to garnish

FOR THE MISO

2 tbsp white miso

1½ tsp brown rice vinegar

1 tsp grated fresh ginger

1 Place 2 cups of water in a large, lidded saucepan and add a pinch of salt. Bring to a boil, then slowly stir in the buckwheat. Reduce the heat to a simmer, cover, and cook for 15 minutes. Then remove from the heat, cover, and leave to stand.

2 Meanwhile, heat the canola oil in a large frying pan over medium heat. Add the chiles and cook for about 2 minutes, stirring, until fragrant. Add the garlic, ginger, and sesame oil, if using, and cook for 2 minutes, stirring frequently. Then add the eggplant and zucchini and cook for another 8–10 minutes, stirring frequently, until the vegetables are cooked through.

3 Meanwhile, for the miso, place all the ingredients in a bowl, add 1 teaspoon of water, and mix until well combined. Stir the mixture into the vegetables and mix well to coat. Then add the kale and cook for another 2–3 minutes, until just wilted. Remove from the heat and sprinkle in the basil and sesame seeds. Serve hot over the buckwheat.

dried red chiles

SWEET AND SPICY SALMON AND QUINOA STIR-FRY

Tender salmon fillets, marinated in a sweet orange juice and honey mixture, are beautifully paired with a rich and spicy stir-fry sauce, nutty quinoa, and fresh greens to make a flavor-packed and filling dinner.

SERVES 2 · PREP 10 MINS, PLUS COOLING AND MARINATING · COOK 40 MINS

2 salmon fillets, about 5½oz (150g) each

⅔ cup uncooked quinoa

1 tbsp light olive oil

1 head of bok choy, white core removed and leaves sliced into ribbons

7oz (200g) bean sprouts

FOR THE MARINADE

1 cup orange juice

¼ cup honey

½ tsp dried chile flakes

1 tbsp soy sauce

1 For the marinade, place all the ingredients in a large saucepan and bring to a boil over medium-high heat. Then reduce the heat to a simmer and cook for about 8–10 minutes until the liquid has reduced. Remove from the heat and leave to cool.

2 Place the salmon in a large plastic bag and pour the marinade over it. Seal the bag, place in the fridge, and leave to marinate for about 2 hours or overnight.

3 Preheat the oven to 400°F (200°C). Remove the salmon from the bag and place each one in the middle of a square sheet of foil. Roll up the sides to make baskets and pour any remaining marinade over the steaks. Continue to roll up the sides to seal the parcels and place them on a baking sheet. Bake for about 20 minutes or until the salmon is cooked.

4 Meanwhile, rinse the quinoa under running water and place in a large saucepan. Add 1 cup of water and bring to a simmer over medium heat. Cook for about 15 minutes or until all the liquid has been absorbed and the grain is fluffy.

5 Heat the oil in a large frying pan over high heat. Add the bok choy and bean sprouts and cook for 3–4 minutes. Then add the cooked quinoa, mix well, and remove from the heat. Divide the quinoa and vegetable mixture between two plates. Place the salmon steaks on top and pour any remaining juices from the foil parcels over them. Serve hot.

PORK, APRiCOT, AND LEEK STiR-FRY WiTH FREEKEH

The sweetness of the apricot in this dish complements the rich and savory flavors of the freekeh and tamari sauce. Pairing the pork with this tantalizing combination results in a truly satisfying meal.

SERVES 4 · PREP 15 MiNS, PLUS MARiNATiNG · COOK 1 HR 10 MiNS

1lb 5oz (600g) pork loin, sliced into long, thin pieces

1 cup uncooked freekeh

3 tbsp vegetable oil

1 leek, about 5½oz (150g), cut into ¼in (5mm) rounds

2 apricots, about 5oz (140g), pitted and thinly sliced

1 garlic clove, thinly sliced

FOR THE MARiNADE

¼ cup tamari sauce or soy sauce

¼ cup toasted sesame oil

2 garlic cloves, crushed

½ tsp sugar

1 For the marinade, place all the ingredients in a large bowl and whisk to combine. Add the pork and mix to coat. Transfer to the fridge and leave to marinate for 20–30 minutes.

2 Meanwhile, place the freekeh in a large, lidded saucepan. Pour in 1 quart of water and bring to a boil. Then, reduce the heat to a simmer, cover, and cook for about 45 minutes or until chewy. Remove from the heat and drain any remaining water. Cover and set aside.

3 Heat 2 tablespoons of the oil in a large frying pan over medium heat. Add the leeks and cook for about 5 minutes, stirring frequently, until softened. Remove with a slotted spoon, place on a plate, and set aside. Then add the apricots to the pan and sauté for about 2 minutes or until just starting to soften, but not brown. Remove from the pan and set aside with the leeks.

4 Pour the remaining oil into the pan, add the garlic, and cook for 1–2 minutes. Then add the pork and marinade and cook, stirring frequently, for about 5 minutes or until the pork just starts to brown. Return the leeks and apricots to the pan and cook, stirring frequently, for another 5 minutes or until the pork is lightly browned all over and cooked through. Remove from the heat. Serve immediately, along with the freekeh.

MiLLET CASHEW STiR-FRY
WiTH CHiLE AND LiME SAUCE

This simple stir-fry is light, yet full of flavor and color. The lime gives it an added zing that pairs well with the sweetness of the toasted cashews and crunchy vegetables.

SERVES 2 · PREP 20 MiNS · COOK 20 MiNS

½ cup uncooked millet

½ cup cashew nuts

2 tbsp olive oil

4oz (115g) carrot, coarsely chopped

4oz (115g) cabbage, coarsely chopped

3½oz (100g) bean sprouts

3oz (85g) red onion, thinly sliced

FOR THE SAUCE

juice of 1 lime and grated zest of ½ lime

2 tbsp soy sauce

2 tbsp honey

1 red chile, seeded and finely chopped

1 Place the millet in a large saucepan. Cover with ½ cup of water and simmer for about 10 minutes or until all the water has been absorbed. Then remove from the heat and set aside.

2 Heat a large wok or frying pan over high heat. Add the cashew nuts and toast until lightly colored. Remove from the heat and coarsely chop. Add the oil to the pan. Then add the carrots, cabbage, bean sprouts, and onions. Cook, stirring frequently, for about 5 minutes or until lightly cooked.

3 Meanwhile, for the sauce, place all the ingredients in a bowl and mix to combine. Add the millet to the vegetables and mix well. Pour over the chile and lime sauce, mix well, and cook for 1–2 minutes. Remove from the heat and serve hot.

GRAiN EXCHANGE

For a variation, try replacing the millet with the same amount of quinoa. Or you could use ¾ cup of bulgur wheat and cook it in about 2½ cups of water.

quinoa

bulgur wheat

POBLANOS STUFFED WITH SPICY SORGHUM AND BLACK BEAN STIR-FRY

Green poblano peppers have a sweet and mild heat that makes them the perfect companion for this well-spiced sorghum stir-fry. An impressive dish, and it's also easy to make.

SERVES 6 · PREP 10 MINUTES, PLUS COOLING · COOK 1 HR 20 MINUTES

½ cup uncooked sorghum

2 cups vegetable stock

6 large poblano peppers

2 tbsp sunflower oil

salt and freshly ground black pepper

1 small red onion, coarsely chopped

3 garlic cloves, crushed

1 tsp chili powder

1 tsp oregano

½ tsp ground cumin

¼ tsp cayenne pepper

14oz (400g) can black beans, drained and rinsed

5½oz (150g) plum tomatoes, seeded and diced

5½oz (150g) can corn kernels

1 tbsp freshly grated Cheddar cheese, to serve

1 Place the sorghum and stock in a small, lidded saucepan and bring to a boil. Then reduce to a simmer, cover, and cook for about 45 minutes. Remove from the heat and leave, covered, for another 10 minutes. Then drain any remaining water and set aside.

2 Meanwhile, preheat the oven to 450°F (230°C). Place the poblano peppers on a lined baking sheet. Brush with half of the oil and season with salt and pepper. Place in the oven and roast for 15–20 minutes, until they start to brown and are tender. Remove from the heat and leave to cool slightly. Once cool enough to handle, slit the peppers in the center, lengthwise, and remove the seeds.

3 Heat the remaining oil in a large cast-iron pan over medium heat. Add the onions and sauté for 5–8 minutes, or until softened. Then add the garlic, chili powder, oregano, cumin, and cayenne pepper. Mix to combine and cook for 2–3 minutes, stirring frequently.

4 Add the sorghum, beans, and tomatoes and stir to combine. Cook for 5 minutes, stirring occasionally. Then add the corn and cook for another 2–3 minutes. Taste, and adjust the seasoning if needed. Spoon the stir-fry mixture into the poblano peppers and scatter any extra on the plates. Garnish with the cheese and serve immediately.

SWEET AND SOUR CHICKEN WITH KAMUT

A different take on the popular sweet and sour chicken, this recipe adds kamut to the traditional Chinese dish for a nuttier flavor and a new wholesome texture.

SERVES 2–3 · PREP 15 MINS, PLUS OVERNIGHT SOAKING · COOK 55 MINS

½ cup uncooked kamut

2 tbsp cornstarch

14½oz (425g) can pineapple chunks in juice, juice reserved

2 tbsp rice wine vinegar

3 tbsp honey

2 tbsp tomato paste

2 tbsp soy sauce, plus extra if needed

1 tbsp canola oil

2 skinless chicken breasts, cut into bite-sized pieces

1 small onion, coarsely chopped

1 red bell pepper, seeded and cut into chunks

2½oz (75g) baby corn, cut into quarters

salt and freshly ground black pepper

1 Place the kamut in a large bowl and cover with water. Leave to soak for about 8 hours or for up to 24 hours. Drain any remaining water. Rinse under running water and drain well.

2 Place the kamut in a saucepan and cover with water. Bring to a boil, then reduce the heat to a simmer. Cover and cook for 40–45 minutes or until tender. Drain and set aside.

3 Meanwhile, mix the cornstarch with 3 tablespoons of the pineapple juice in a small bowl. Then add the vinegar, honey, tomato paste, soy sauce, and remaining pineapple juice. Mix until well combined.

4 Heat the oil in a large frying pan over medium-high heat. Add the chicken and cook for about 3 minutes, stirring frequently, until lightly colored. Then add the onions, red bell peppers, and corn. Cook for 3 minutes, stirring frequently, until the onions are translucent.

5 Add the pineapple and cornstarch mixture and bring to a boil. Then reduce the heat to a simmer and cook for 2–3 minutes, until the sauce has thickened and the chicken has cooked through. Taste, adjust the seasoning if needed, and add more soy sauce if required. Serve the kamut topped with the chicken and vegetables.

GRAIN EXCHANGE

This dish works really well with a variety of similar grains. For a variation, try replacing the kamut with the same amount of any of the following grains and see p16–17 for advice on cooking times.

spelt

barley

wheat berries

why not try...

Instead of chicken, you could use the same amount of **duck breast,** or one **skinless turkey breast,** or 8oz (225g) of **pork loin.**

AMARANTH-CRUSTED TOFU
WiTH GREEN BEANS AND BLACK RiCE

This vegetarian dish uses coarse amaranth flour and sesame seeds in place of bread crumbs to coat tender tofu, giving it a crunchy, nutty texture, and pairs it with a spicy, salty green bean stir-fry.

SERVES 4 · PREP 15 MiNS · COOK 50 MiNS

1⅔ cups black rice

14oz (400g) extra firm tofu, drained

¼ cup amaranth flour

3 tbsp sesame seeds, plus extra to serve

1 egg, lightly beaten

salt and freshly ground black pepper

2–3 tbsp canola oil

2 tbsp sesame oil, plus extra to serve

1 onion, thinly sliced

1 tsp grated fresh ginger

3 mild red chiles, seeded and sliced into ½in (1cm) pieces

3 garlic cloves, crushed and thinly sliced

7oz (200g) green beans, blanched

1 tbsp tamari sauce, plus extra to serve

2 scallions, cut into 1in (2.5cm) long pieces

1 Place the rice in a large saucepan and cook according to package instructions. Remove from the heat, cover, and set aside. Pat the tofu dry with paper towels and cut 16 x 1in (2.5cm) thick triangles. Set aside.

2 Place the amaranth flour and sesame seeds in a shallow dish and mix to combine. Place the egg in a small bowl. Season the tofu with salt and pepper and brush lightly with the egg. Then toss the tofu in the amaranth flour mixture until lightly coated.

3 Heat the canola oil in a large frying pan over medium-low heat. Once the oil has heated, reduce the heat to low and add the tofu. Cook for 3–4 minutes on each side, turning the tofu gently to prevent it breaking apart, until evenly browned on each side. Remove with a slotted spoon, set aside on a lined plate, and keep warm. Drain the excess oil from the pan.

4 Add the sesame oil to the pan and increase the heat to medium. Add the onions, ginger, and chiles. Cook for about 5 minutes, stirring frequently, until softened. Then add the garlic and cook for another minute. Add the green beans and cook, stirring, for 3–4 minutes.

5 Add the tamari sauce and scallions. Season with pepper and cook, stirring, for about 3 minutes. Add the tofu and gently heat through for 2 minutes. Do not stir the tofu as it may break apart. Remove from the heat. Divide the rice between four serving plates. Top with the green bean and onion stir-fry and the tofu. Sprinkle with sesame seeds, drizzle with some oil and tamari sauce on top, and serve warm.

BEEF AND EDAMAME STiR-FRY

In this quick and easy recipe, tender sirloin steak is stir-fried with a homemade sauce and fresh vegetables. Served over whole-grain freekeh, it makes for a healthy alternative to the traditional beef stir-fry.

SERVES 4 · PREP 10 MiNS · COOK 25 MiNS

1¼ cups uncooked freekeh

1 tbsp olive oil

1lb (450g) beef sirloin steak, cut into strips

8oz (225g) carrots, shredded

8oz (225g) frozen shelled edamame

⅔ cup low-sodium soy sauce

¼ cup beef stock

¼ cup rice vinegar

½ tbsp cornstarch, mixed with a little warm water

1 tsp freshly grated ginger

½ tsp freshly ground black pepper

handful of chopped scallions, to garnish

1 Place the freekeh and 3 cups of water in a large, lidded saucepan over medium heat. Bring to a boil, then reduce the heat to a simmer. Cover and cook for 20–25 minutes, until almost all the water has been absorbed. Remove from the heat, drain any excess water, and set aside.

2 Meanwhile, heat the oil in a large, lidded frying pan over medium heat. Add the beef and cook for about 1 minute, stirring occasionally. Remove with a slotted spoon and set aside. Add the carrots and edamame to the pan, cover, and cook for about 5 minutes, stirring occasionally.

3 Place the soy sauce, beef stock, rice vinegar, cornstarch, ginger, and pepper in a bowl. Whisk until well combined. Pour the liquid mixture into the pan. Then add the beef, stir well to combine, and bring to a boil. Cook, stirring frequently, for another 10–12 minutes or until the sauce thickens slightly. Remove from the heat. Divide the freekeh between four serving bowls and top with the stir-fry. Serve hot, garnished with scallions.

EGG-FRIED MILLET

Wholesome and fluffy millet replaces the standard rice in this egg-fried classic.

SERVES 2 · PREP 10 MINS · COOK 30 MINS

½ cup uncooked millet	3½oz (100g) bean sprouts
2 eggs	2½oz (75g) frozen peas, defrosted
1 tsp sesame oil	2 tsp soy sauce
2 tbsp olive oil	
4 scallions, chopped into rounds	

1 Place the millet in a large saucepan, cover with ½ cup of water, and bring to a boil. Then reduce the heat to a simmer and cook for 10 minutes or until the millet is tender and fluffy. Remove from the heat and use a fork to fluff up the millet. Set aside to cool.

2 Place the eggs and sesame oil in a bowl, whisk to combine, and set aside. Heat the olive oil in a frying pan. Add the millet and cook for 3 minutes, stirring constantly. Then add the scallions, bean sprouts, and peas. Cook, stirring frequently, for another 3 minutes.

3 Move the millet and vegetables to one side of the pan and add the egg mixture. Cook for 1–2 minutes, without stirring, until it is set. Then use a wooden spoon to break up the egg and mix with the millet and vegetables.

4 Cook, stirring frequently, for about 3 minutes or until the egg is fully cooked and well combined. Remove from the heat. Add the soy sauce and mix well. Season to taste, if needed, and serve hot.

CHINESE CHICKEN WITH BROCCOLI OVER KAMUT

This popular Chinese dish gets a makeover with the addition of protein-rich kamut.

SERVES 4 · PREP 10 MINS, PLUS SOAKING · COOK 50 MINS

	FOR THE SAUCE
1 cup uncooked kamut	½ cup low-sodium soy sauce
1 tbsp canola oil	¾ cups chicken stock
1lb (450g) chicken breasts, cut into ¼in (5mm) thick strips	2 tbsp cornstarch
4¾oz (130g) broccoli, steamed	2 tsp ground ginger
1 tsp freshly ground black pepper	1 tbsp sesame oil

1 Place the kamut in a large bowl and cover with water. Leave to soak for 8 hours. Then drain, rinse under running water, and drain again.

2 Place the kamut in a large saucepan, cover with 3 cups of water, and bring to a boil. Reduce the heat to medium-low and cook for 45 minutes or until tender. Then remove from the heat and drain any remaining water. Set aside.

3 For the sauce, place all the ingredients in a bowl and whisk to combine. Heat the oil in a large frying pan over medium heat. Add the chicken and cook for about 5 minutes, turning over once or twice, until no longer pink on the outside.

4 Add the broccoli and sauce to the pan and season with the pepper. Cover and cook for about 7 minutes or until the sauce has thickened. Remove from the heat. Serve the kamut hot, topped with the chicken and broccoli.

VEGETABLE-FRIED FARRO

In this whole grain twist on the classic stir-fry recipe, farro replaces the usual starchy white rice. Its flavor is deepened by the fact that is toasted first, before being cooked as normal.

SERVES 3 · PREP 15 MINS · COOK 30 MINS

1 tbsp extra virgin olive oil

¾ cup cracked farro

1 garlic clove, sliced

salt

FOR THE VEGETABLES

2 tbsp canola oil

1 garlic clove, crushed

1 tsp grated fresh ginger

3 scallions, thinly sliced

1 carrot, finely diced

1 red bell pepper, seeded and finely diced

3½oz (100g) sugar snap peas

2 tbsp tamari or low-sodium soy sauce

1 large egg, lightly beaten

1 Heat the olive oil in a saucepan over medium heat. Add the farro and garlic, season with salt, and cook for 5 minutes, stirring frequently. Then add 1 quart of water and bring to a boil. Reduce the heat to a simmer, cover, and cook for 20 minutes. Remove from the heat, drain any remaining water, and set aside.

2 For the vegetables, heat 1 tablespoon of the canola oil in a large frying pan over medium heat. Add the garlic, ginger, and onions and cook for 2 minutes, stirring frequently. Then add the carrots, bell peppers, peas, and 1 tablespoon of the tamari. Mix well and cook for 3–4 minutes or until the vegetables are just softened.

3 Move the vegetables to the side and pour in the egg. Cook the egg for 2 minutes, stirring frequently. Then stir to mix the egg with the vegetables. Add the farro and the remaining oil and tamari. Cook for another 2 minutes, stirring frequently. Remove from the heat and serve hot.

sugar snap peas

TURKEY AND BALSAMIC STIR-FRY WITH FARRO

Full of Mediterranean flavors, this dish is light yet satisfying. The stir-fried vegetables add a refreshing crunch, complementing the nuttiness of the farro and the tender and subtle taste of the marinated turkey.

SERVES 3 · PREP 10 MINS, PLUS SOAKING AND MARINATING · COOK 55 MINS

½ cup uncooked farro

2 turkey steaks, about 4½oz (125g) each, sliced into ¾in (2cm) wide strips

1 red or orange bell pepper, seeded and cut into strips

1 red onion, coarsely chopped

1 zucchini, sliced into rounds

1 tbsp olive oil

handful of basil leaves, to serve

FOR THE MARINADE

3 tbsp balsamic vinegar

1½ tbsp olive oil

1 garlic clove, finely chopped

1 tsp mixed Italian seasoning

pinch of salt

1 Place the farro in a large bowl and cover with water. Leave to soak for 8 hours or up to 24 hours. Then drain any remaining water and rinse under running water. Drain well and set aside.

2 For the marinade, place all the ingredients in a small bowl and mix to combine. Place the turkey in a plastic bag. Place the red bell peppers, onions, and zucchini in a separate plastic bag. Divide the marinade equally between the two bags. Then seal the bags and shake lightly to coat. Place in the fridge to marinate for at least 2 hours.

3 Meanwhile, place the farro in a saucepan and cover with water. Bring to a boil, then reduce the heat to a simmer, and cover. Cook for 30–40 minutes or until tender. Remove from the heat and set aside.

4 Heat the oil in a large saucepan over medium-high heat. Add the turkey, reserving the marinade. Cook, stirring frequently, for about 3 minutes or until cooked through. Then add the vegetables, reserving the marinade. Cook, stirring frequently, for 5 minutes, making sure they stay crunchy and do not overcook.

5 Increase the heat to high. Add all of the reserved marinade to the pan and cook for 3 minutes, stirring frequently, until reduced to a sticky glaze. Add a splash of water if it starts to stick to the bottom. Reduce the heat, add the farro, and stir well to combine. Remove from the heat, garnish with basil, and serve hot.

BEEF, BROCCOLI, AND COCONUT STIR-FRY WITH BULGUR WHEAT

A flavorsome dish that combines beef with creamy bulgur wheat and crunchy broccoli.

SERVES 2 · PREP 10 MINS · COOK 20 MINS

¾ cup uncooked bulgur wheat	7oz (200g) broccoli, cut into small florets
1 tbsp vegetable or coconut oil	⅓ cup full-fat coconut milk
1in (2.5cm) piece of fresh ginger, finely chopped	2 tbsp soy sauce, plus extra if needed
10oz (300g) steak, cut into strips	salt and freshly ground black pepper

1 Place the bulgur wheat in a large, lidded saucepan. Add 2½ cups of water and bring to a boil. Then reduce the heat to a simmer, cover, and cook for 15 minutes or until all the water has been absorbed and the bulgur wheat is tender.

2 Heat the oil in a large frying pan over medium heat. Add the ginger and sauté for 3 minutes. Add the beef and cook for 5 minutes, stirring occasionally. Then add the broccoli, mix well, and cook for 3–5 minutes, stirring frequently. Add the bulgur wheat, coconut milk, and soy sauce and mix well.

3 Cook for 2–3 minutes, stirring frequently, until the beef is cooked through and some of the milk has been absorbed. Make sure the broccoli is still crunchy. Season to taste, if needed, and add more soy sauce if required. Remove from the heat. Drizzle with soy sauce and serve immediately.

PINEAPPLE AND PORK STIR-FRY

This recipes brings together pork, pineapple, and millet in a great combination of Asian flavors.

SERVES 4 · PREP 10 MINS · COOK 30 MINS

1 cup uncooked millet	1 tbsp cornstarch
4oz (115g) carrots, sliced into batons	2 tsp olive oil
4oz (115g) snow peas	1in (2.5cm) piece of fresh ginger, grated
¼ cup low-sodium vegetable stock, plus extra if needed	2 garlic cloves, crushed
	5 scallions, chopped
2 tbsp low-sodium soy sauce	1lb (450g) boneless pork chops, cut into thin strips
2 tbsp seasoned rice vinegar	4oz (115g) pineapple, chopped

1 Place 2 cups of water in a large, lidded saucepan and bring to a boil. Then stir in the millet, cover, and reduce the heat to medium-low. Cook for 15 minutes, until almost all the water has been absorbed. Remove from the heat.

2 Place the carrots and peas in a steamer and steam for 10 minutes or until softened. Remove and set aside. For the sauce, place the stock, soy sauce, rice vinegar, and cornstarch in a bowl. Whisk until well combined and set aside.

3 Heat the oil in a large frying pan over medium-high heat. Add the ginger, garlic, and scallions and cook for 1 minute, stirring occasionally. Then add the pork and cook for 5–6 minutes, stirring occasionally, until well browned. Pour the sauce in and stir to coat. Stir in the peas and carrots.

4 Cook for 2–3 minutes, adding more stock if needed, until the sauce thickens and coats the back of a spoon. Stir in the pineapple and remove from the heat. Serve hot over the millet.

TOFU AND KAMUT STIR-FRY

Meaty tofu makes a great vegan alternative in this nutty stir-fry, while the vegetables add lots of crunchy texture and the marinade offers a sweet and sour piquancy.

SERVES 2 · PREP 15 MINS, PLUS MARINATING AND SOAKING · COOK 1 HR

14oz (400g) firm tofu, drained

½ cup uncooked kamut

3 tbsp vegetable oil

1 carrot, cut into matchsticks

1 red bell pepper, seeded and cut into thin slices

1¾oz (50g) bean sprouts

4 scallions, thinly sliced

salt and freshly ground black pepper

FOR THE MARINADE

¼ cup soy sauce, plus extra if needed

2 tbsp honey

2in (5cm) piece of fresh ginger, finely chopped

2 garlic cloves, finely chopped

1 For the marinade, place all the ingredients in a bowl and mix to combine. Cut the tofu into ¾in (2cm) cubes and place in a plastic bag. Pour half the marinade over, seal the bag, and shake lightly to coat. Leave to marinate in the fridge for 3–4 hours. Reserve the remaining marinade

2 Place the kamut in a large bowl, cover with water, and leave to soak for 8 hours. Then drain and rinse under running water. Drain and place in a large, lidded saucepan. Cover with water and bring to a boil. Then reduce the heat to a simmer, cover, and cook for 45 minutes or until tender. Remove from the heat and drain.

3 Heat 2 tablespoons of the oil in a frying pan over medium-high heat. Add the tofu and sauté for about 10 minutes, until evenly browned. Remove with a slotted spoon. Pour the remaining oil into the pan. Add the carrots and red bell peppers and cook for about 2 minutes, stirring frequently.

4 Add the bean sprouts and cook for about 3 minutes, stirring frequently. Add the kamut, tofu, and reserved marinade and combine well. Then add the onions and cook for 2 minutes, stirring frequently. Season to taste, adding more soy sauce if needed, and remove from the heat. Serve hot.

GRAIN EXCHANGE
You could replace the kamut with any of the following grains. Use the same amount of grain.

wheat berries

spelt

barley

why not try...

You could try adding the same amount of **chicken** instead of the tofu or use the same quantity of **yellow bell peppers** in place of the red bell peppers.

SHRIMP AND ASPARAGUS STIR-FRY WITH POLENTA

In this satisfying dish, shrimp and asparagus are stir-fried in a light white wine sauce and served over creamy, cheesy polenta. Quick and easy, it is perfect for dinner or even impressing your friends!

SERVES 4 · PREP 10 MINS · COOK 20 MINS

2 tbsp extra virgin olive oil

3 garlic cloves, crushed

6–8 scallions, white and green parts, finely chopped

1lb (450g) asparagus, ends removed and cut into 1in (2.5cm) pieces

1lb (450g) shrimp, peeled and deveined

¼ cup white wine

salt and freshly ground black pepper

1 cup uncooked polenta

1 cup freshly grated Asiago or Parmesan cheese, plus extra to garnish

1 lemon, sliced, to serve

1 Heat the oil in a large frying pan over medium heat. Add the garlic, scallions, and asparagus. Cook for 5 minutes, stirring occasionally, until the onions have softened. Then add the shrimp and cook for 3 minutes, stirring, until just beginning to turn pink.

2 Pour in the wine and stir to combine. Cook for another 2–3 minutes or until the shrimp are cooked through and pink. Remove from the heat and season to taste if needed.

3 Meanwhile, place 3 cups of water and ¼ teaspoon salt in a large saucepan and bring to a boil. Stir in the polenta and reduce the heat to medium-low. Cook for about 5 minutes, stirring occasionally. Remove from the heat and stir in the cheese.

4 Divide the polenta evenly between four plates and top with one-quarter of the shrimp and asparagus stir-fry. Garnish with cheese and serve hot with lemon slices.

NOURISHING RISOTTOS AND PILAFS

ÌTALIAN TOMATO BARLEY RÌSOTTO

Bursting with italian flavors, this healthy risotto gets its interesting texture from slow-cooked pearl barley. The green olives and basil leaves also make great additions to the traditional tomato sauce.

SERVES 4 · PREP 10 MiNS · COOK 45 MiNS

1 tbsp olive oil

1 onion, finely chopped

2 garlic cloves, crushed

1½ cups pearl barley, rinsed

1½ cups tomato sauce

2⅔ cups vegetable stock

1 tsp Italian seasoning

14oz (400g) can cannellini beans, drained

4¼oz (120g) green olives, pitted and halved

salt and freshly ground black pepper

handful of basil leaves, to garnish

1 Heat the oil in a large, lidded saucepan over medium-high heat. Add the onions and garlic and cook for about 5 minutes or until the onions are softened. Then add the barley to the pan, stir to coat with the oil, and cook for another 2 minutes.

2 Add the passata, stock, and Italian seasoning to the pan. Stir well and reduce the heat to a simmer. Cover and cook for 30 minutes or until most of the liquid has been absorbed and the barley is chewy. Make sure you stir the risotto occasionally to prevent the barley from sticking to the bottom of the pan.

3 Stir the beans into the risotto and cook for another 5 minutes. Remove from the heat and stir in the olives, making sure they are evenly distributed. Season to taste, garnish with basil leaves, and serve hot.

GRAIN EXCHANGE
You can use the same amount of any one of the following grains in place of the barley.

wheat berries

spelt

farro

why not try...
Try the same amount of **navy beans, chickpeas,** or **borlotti beans** instead of the cannellini beans.

TEFF AND BUTTERNUT SQUASH RISOTTO

The sweetness of roasted butternut squash combines with aromatic sage and rich heavy cream in this classic risotto that uses teff in place of the more usual rice. it's a deliciously warming dish for a cool fall day.

SERVES 2 · PREP 20 MINS · COOK 1 HR 10 MINS

1 butternut squash, about 1lb 2oz (500g), seeded and diced into ½–¾in (1–2cm) pieces

2 tbsp olive oil

1 tbsp unsalted butter

1 small onion, finely chopped

1 garlic clove, finely chopped

½ cup uncooked teff

2 cups chicken stock

2 tbsp heavy cream

3 tbsp freshly grated Parmesan cheese, plus extra to serve

¼ tsp dried sage

salt and freshly ground black pepper

2 tbsp chopped basil, to garnish

1 Preheat the oven to 400°F (200°C). Place the butternut squash on a large baking sheet, drizzle 1 tablespoon of the oil on top, and toss to coat. Place the tray in the oven and bake for about 40 minutes or until the squash is tender but still has some bite to it.

2 Heat the butter and remaining oil in a large frying pan over medium heat. Add the onions and garlic and sauté for about 5 minutes or until the onions are soft and translucent. Then add the teff and stir to coat in the butter and oil.

3 Add 1 cup of the stock, a ladleful at a time, stirring constantly, allowing the liquid to be fully absorbed before adding more. Then add half of the butternut squash and stir to mix.

4 Pour in the remaining stock, a little at a time, stirring constantly. Cook for 15–20 minutes, until all the stock has been absorbed and the squash has started to break down. Then add the cream and Parmesan and stir to mix.

5 Add the sage and remaining butternut squash to the pan and stir to mix. Remove from the heat and season to taste. Garnish the risotto with basil and Parmesan and serve hot.

GARLICKY SPINACH AND SPELT RISOTTO

Easy to make and quick to prepare, this hearty risotto contains the goodness of spinach, garlic, and whole grain spelt and is a great nutrient boost for when you're feeling a little under the weather.

SERVES 2 · PREP 10 MINS · COOK 30 MINS

1 tbsp olive oil

1 tbsp unsalted butter

1 small onion, finely chopped

4 garlic cloves, finely chopped

½ cup pearled spelt

2 cups hot chicken stock

3oz (85g) spinach, rough stems removed and coarsely chopped

2 tbsp heavy cream

3 tbsp freshly grated Parmesan cheese, plus extra to serve

1 Heat the oil and butter in a large frying pan over medium heat. Add the onions and garlic and sauté for about 5 minutes or until the onions are translucent. Then add the spelt, stir to coat in the oil and butter, and sauté for another 3 minutes.

2 Add the stock, a ladleful at a time, stirring constantly, allowing the liquid to be fully absorbed before adding more. Cook for 10 minutes, stirring frequently, until three-quarters of the liquid has been absorbed. Then add the spinach, a handful at a time, letting it wilt and reduce with the stock before adding more.

3 Cook, stirring frequently, for another 10 minutes, until all the stock has been absorbed and the spinach has wilted. Then add the cream and Parmesan, stir well to combine, and season to taste. Remove from the heat. Sprinkle some Parmesan over the top and serve hot.

GRAIN EXCHANGE

For a change, try replacing the spelt with the same amount of either of the following grains.

barley

wheat berries

APPLE, WALNUT, GOJI BERRY, CHICKEN, AND WHEAT BERRY PILAF

This filling pilaf uniquely combines crisp apple and chewy wheat berries with nuts and sweet berries. Add some tender chicken to the mix and you're left with a healthy and filling meal.

SERVES 4 · PREP 15 MINS, PLUS SOAKING · COOK 50 MINS

1 cup uncooked
   wheat berries

⅓ cup goji berries

¼ cup walnuts, chopped

1 tbsp olive oil

2 chicken breasts, diced

1 onion, finely sliced

1 garlic clove, crushed

1 large apple, grated

salt

handful of flat-leaf parsley,
   finely chopped

handful of basil leaves,
   finely chopped

1 Place the wheat berries in a large saucepan, cover with water, and bring to a boil. Then reduce the heat to a simmer and cook for 30–40 minutes or until they are tender.

2 Meanwhile, place the goji berries in a small bowl, cover with water, and leave to soak for 10 minutes. Heat a large frying pan over medium heat. Add the walnuts and lightly toast for 3–4 minutes. Remove from the heat and set aside.

3 Increase the heat to medium-high and pour the oil into the pan. Add the chicken and cook for 10 minutes, stirring frequently. Then add the onions and garlic to the pan. Cook for another 5 minutes, stirring occasionally, until the chicken is cooked through and the onions have softened. Remove from the heat.

4 Drain the wheat berries, add them to the pan, and mix to combine with the chicken and onions. Drain the goji berries and discard the water. Add the goji berries, walnuts, and apples to the pilaf and mix lightly to combine. Taste and adjust the seasoning, if needed. Garnish with the herbs and serve hot.

GRAIN EXCHANGE

For a change, try using the same amount of any one of the following grains in place of the wheat berries.

barley

spelt

farro

why not try ...

Instead of the goji berries, try some **dried cranberries**, or swap **pecans** for the walnuts. You could even try adding turkey instead of the chicken.

SWEET POTATO, CRANBERRY, AND PECAN FARRO

A fall-inspired recipe, this pilaf-like dish is packed with the rich flavor of sweet potato, which is well paired with the nutty and creamy farro, crunchy pecans, and tangy apple cider dressing.

SERVES 4 · PREP 15 MINS, PLUS OVERNIGHT SOAKING · COOK 1 HR 10 MINS

1 cup uncooked farro

2 sweet potatoes, cut into ½in (1cm) cubes

2 tbsp olive oil

1 onion, finely chopped

1 tsp ground cinnamon

½ tsp ground cumin

¾ cup dried cranberries

1 cup pecans, coarsely chopped

¼ cup coarsely chopped flat-leaf parsley

FOR THE DRESSING

3 tbsp extra virgin olive oil

1 tbsp apple cider vinegar

1 Place the farro in a bowl and cover with water. Leave to soak overnight or for up to 8 hours. Then drain, rinse under running water, and drain well again.

2 Place the farro in a large, lidded saucepan, cover with water, and bring to a boil. Then reduce the heat to a simmer, cover, and cook for 30 minutes, until tender. Remove from the heat and drain any remaining water. Set aside.

3 Meanwhile, preheat the oven to 400°F (200°C). Place the potatoes on a baking sheet and toss with 1 tablespoon of the oil. Bake for 30–40 minutes, until tender.

4 Heat the remaining oil in a large frying pan over medium heat. Add the onions and cook for about 5 minutes, stirring frequently, until softened. Then add the cinnamon and cumin and cook for another 2 minutes, stirring frequently.

5 Add the farro and sweet potatoes and stir to combine. Then add the cranberries, stir to mix, and cook for another 2 minutes, stirring frequently. Remove from the heat.

6 For the dressing, combine the ingredients in a small bowl and pour over the pilaf. Toss to mix, sprinkle in the pecans and parsley, and serve hot.

GRAIN EXCHANGE

Try replacing the farro with the same amount of either of the following grains.

spelt

barley

GOAT CHEESE, BALSAMIC VINEGAR, AND BUCKWHEAT RISOTTO
WITH PROSCIUTTO

Buckwheat makes a delicious and healthy substitute for rice in this risotto. The pairing of creamy melted goat cheese with tangy balsamic vinegar proves to be a real treat for the taste buds.

SERVES 2 · PREP 15 MINS · COOK 30 MINS

3 tbsp olive oil

2 garlic cloves, crushed

1 onion, diced

1 cup uncooked buckwheat

3 cups chicken stock

3 tbsp butter

salt and freshly ground
   black pepper

¼ cup goat cheese

1 tbsp balsamic vinegar

5 slices prosciutto, chopped

1 tbsp coarsely chopped
   flat-leaf parsley

1 Heat the oil in a large saucepan over medium heat. Add the garlic and the onions and cook for 3–4 minutes, stirring frequently, until softened. Then add the buckwheat and cook for another 2 minutes, stirring frequently.

2 Pour in the stock, stir to mix, and bring to a boil. Then reduce the heat to a simmer and cook for about 15 minutes, stirring frequently. Then add the butter and mix well to combine. Cook for another 5 minutes, until almost all of the stock has been absorbed. Add more stock or water to the risotto if it starts to become dry too quickly.

3 Remove from the heat and season to taste. Add the goat cheese and vinegar and mix until the cheese has melted and is well incorporated. Sprinkle in the prosciutto and parsley and stir to mix. Serve hot.

CHERRY AND PISTACHIO FREEKEH PILAF

This tasty freekeh dish is made with warming, aromatic spices and mixed with dried cherries and pistachios, creating a savory and sweet pilaf unlike any you've had before.

SERVES 4 · PREP 5 MINS · COOK 20–25 MINS

1 cup uncooked freekeh

8 cardamom pods

8 whole cloves

1 tbsp oil

1 onion, finely chopped

1 tsp ground cinnamon

pinch of salt

⅔ cup dried cherries, coarsely chopped

¾ cup pistachios, coarsely chopped

FOR THE DRESSING

3 tbsp olive oil

2 tbsp lemon juice

pinch of salt

1 Place the freekeh in a large saucepan, cover with 1 quart of water, and place over medium heat. Add the cardamom and cloves and simmer for 20 minutes or until all the water has been absorbed. Drain any remaining water and remove and discard the cardamom and cloves. Set aside.

2 Meanwhile, heat the oil in a large frying pan over medium heat. Add the onions and cook for 5–10 minutes, stirring occasionally, until softened and translucent. Then add the cinnamon and cook for another 2 minutes.

3 For the dressing, place all the ingredients in a small bowl and mix to combine. Add the freekeh to the onion mixture, season with the salt, and stir to mix. Then add the cherries and pistachios and stir until evenly distributed. Remove from the heat. Serve hot with the dressing drizzled over the dish.

GRAIN EXCHANGE

For a variation, in place of the freekeh, use ¾ cup of **bulgur wheat** and cook it in 2½ cups of water.

why not try...

Try **apricots** instead of the dried cherries, or **almonds** in place of the pistachios.

NUTTY SPICED BULGUR WHEAT PILAF
WITH RAISINS

Delicately flavored with spices, this light and aromatic pilaf makes the perfect dinner dish. The toasted almonds and raisins add texture and really complement the creamy taste of the bulgur wheat.

SERVES 4 · PREP 10 MINS · COOK 45 MINS

¾ cup uncooked bulgur wheat

⅔ cup flaked almonds

1 tbsp olive oil

1 onion, finely chopped

1 tsp ground cinnamon

2 tbsp ground cumin

⅔ cup raisins

1 cup vegetable stock

salt and freshly ground black pepper

¼ cup chopped flat-leaf parsley, to garnish

1 Place the bulgur wheat in a large saucepan and cover with 2½ cups of water. Bring to a boil, then reduce the heat to a simmer. Cook for 20–30 minutes or until all the water has been absorbed and the bulgur wheat is soft. Remove from the heat, drain any remaining water, and set aside.

2 Heat a nonstick frying pan over medium-high heat. Add the almonds and toast them for about 5 minutes, stirring frequently, until golden brown. Remove from the heat and set aside.

3 Heat the oil in a saucepan over medium heat. Add the onions and cook for about 5 minutes, stirring frequently, until softened. Then add the cinnamon and cumin and cook, stirring frequently, for another 2 minutes.

4 Add the raisins and bulgur wheat and mix well to combine. Cook for another 2 minutes, adding the stock if the mixture gets too dry or sticks to the bottom of the pan. Remove from the heat and season to taste. Sprinkle with the almonds and garnish with parsley. Serve hot.

almonds

MUSHROOM BARLEY RISOTTO

Pearl barley makes a good substitute for rice in this earthy mushroom risotto. Be sure to cook it slowly to get the right texture.

SERVES 4 · PREP 10 MINS · COOK 45 MINS

1 tbsp olive oil	1¼ cups freshly grated Parmesan cheese
1 small onion, diced	1 tbsp finely chopped sage
15 cremini mushrooms, thinly sliced	sea salt and freshly ground black pepper
1 cup uncooked pearl barley	
4fl oz (120ml) white wine	
1 quart hot chicken stock	

1 Heat the oil in a large nonstick frying pan over low heat. Add the onions and mushrooms. Cook, stirring frequently, for about 10 minutes or until the onions are softened and the mushrooms have browned and released their juices.

2 Increase the heat to medium, stir in the barley, and cook for 1 minute. Pour in the wine and cook for 5 minutes or until fully absorbed. Gradually add the stock, a ladleful at a time, stirring constantly, allowing the liquid to be fully absorbed before adding more.

3 Cook for 25–30 minutes, stirring frequently. Then stir in the Parmesan and sage and season to taste. Mix well to combine and remove from the heat. Serve immediately.

PEA AND GOAT CHEESE AMARANTH RISOTTO

A richly flavored risotto made with spring peas, salty goat cheese, and earthy amaranth.

SERVES 2 · PREP 5 MINS · COOK 40 MINS

1 tbsp walnut oil	3 cups hot vegetable stock
1 onion, finely chopped	7oz (200g) frozen peas
1 garlic clove, finely chopped	3 tbsp soft goat cheese
1⅓ cups uncooked amaranth	salt and freshly ground black pepper
¼ cup uncooked teff	

1 Heat the oil in a large nonstick saucepan over medium heat. Add the onions and garlic and cook, stirring frequently, for about 5 minutes or until the onions are softened.

2 Add the amaranth, teff, and stock and stir to combine. Bring to a simmer, then reduce the heat to medium. Cook, stirring frequently, for about 25 minutes.

3 Add the peas and cook for another 10 minutes or until all the stock has been absorbed and the amaranth and teff are soft and creamy. Sprinkle with the cheese and season to taste. Stir well to combine and remove from the heat. Serve hot.

SPICY SHRIMP WITH LIME, FARRO, AND CILANTRO

This refreshing dish makes an ideal dinner, marrying luscious shrimp with creamy avocado, sweet baby plum tomatoes, and nutty farro. The chile flakes and lime juice add just the right amount of piquancy.

SERVES 4 · PREP 10 MINS · COOK 1 HR 10 MINS

1 cup uncooked farro

salt and freshly ground black pepper

2 tbsp olive oil

3 garlic cloves, crushed

1lb (450g) shrimp, peeled and deveined

2 tomatoes, diced

½ tsp chile flakes

1 avocado, pitted and diced

5½ oz (150g) baby plum tomatoes, halved

2 tbsp finely chopped cilantro leaves

¼ cup lime juice

2 lemons or limes, halved, to serve (optional)

1 Place the farro in a large, lidded saucepan. Pour in 2⅓ cups of water and add ½ teaspoon salt. Bring to a boil over medium heat. Then reduce the heat to medium-low, cover, and cook for 50–60 minutes, until tender. Remove from the heat, drain any remaining water, and transfer to a large bowl. Set aside.

2 Meanwhile, heat the oil in a large, lidded frying pan over medium heat. Add the garlic and cook for about 1 minute, stirring, until fragrant. Then add the shrimp, tomatoes, and chile flakes and stir well. Cover, and cook for about 10 minutes or until the shrimp are pink and cooked through. Season to taste and remove from the heat.

3 Add the avocado, baby plum tomatoes, and cilantro to the farro. Mix well to combine. Drizzle the lime juice over and toss lightly to coat. Taste and adjust the seasoning and divide evenly between four plates. Top with the spicy shrimp and serve hot with lemons or limes, if using.

CURRIED SORGHUM PILAF
WITH COCONUT

Cauliflower has been eaten for hundreds of years and became popular during the 16th and 17th centuries, when it was considered a delicacy. Combined with the curry spices and creamy coconut milk, it makes for a great flavor match.

SERVES 2 · PREP 10 MINS · COOK 1 HR 15 MINS

½ cup uncooked sorghum

5½oz (150g) cauliflower, chopped into florets

½ cup coconut flakes

1 tbsp olive oil

1 onion, finely chopped

2 tsp mild curry powder

⅓ cup coconut milk

salt and freshly ground black pepper

2 tbsp chopped cilantro leaves, to garnish

1 Place the sorghum in a large saucepan, cover with water, and bring to a boil. Then reduce the heat to a simmer and cook for 45 minutes—1 hour or until the sorghum is tender, but still chewy. Remove from the heat and set aside.

2 Place the cauliflower in a steamer and steam for 10 minutes or until tender when pierced with a fork. Set aside. Heat a frying pan over medium-high heat. Add the coconut flakes and toast for about 5 minutes, stirring frequently, until lightly toasted. Remove from the heat and set aside.

3 Pour the oil into the pan and reduce the heat to medium. Add the onion and sauté for about 5 minutes or until softened. Then add the curry powder and sauté for about 2 minutes. Add the cauliflower and sorghum and mix well to combine.

4 Add the coconut milk to the pan. Mix well and cook for another 2 minutes. Then add half the coconut flakes and mix well to combine. Season to taste and remove from the heat. Sprinkle in the remaining coconut, garnish with cilantro, and serve hot.

GRAIN EXCHANGE

For a change, try replacing the sorghum with the same amount of either of these grains.

kamut

millet

BACON, KALE, AND BARLEY RISOTTO

The perfect comfort food and packed full of goodness, this risotto is amazingly tasty. The creamy barley makes a great base for the contrast of the salty bacon and the nutrient-rich kale.

SERVES 2 · PREP 15 MINS, PLUS OVERNIGHT SOAKING · COOK 40 MINS

¾ cup uncooked pearl barley

1 tbsp butter, room temperature

1½ tbsp olive oil

1 small onion, finely chopped

1 garlic clove, finely chopped

2 cups hot vegetable stock

1oz (30g) kale, stems removed and coarsely chopped

2 tbsp heavy cream

3 tbsp freshly grated Parmesan cheese, plus extra to serve

4 slices of thick-cut unsmoked bacon, cut into strips

salt and freshly ground black pepper

1 Place the barley in a bowl, cover with water, and leave to soak overnight or for up to 8 hours. Then drain well and rinse under running water. Drain again and set aside.

2 Heat the butter and 1 tablespoon of the oil in a frying pan over medium heat. Add the onions and garlic and sauté for about 5 minutes or until the onions are translucent.

3 Add the barley, stir to coat in the oil and butter, and cook for 3 minutes, stirring frequently. Then add the stock, a ladleful at a time, stirring constantly, allowing the liquid to be fully absorbed before adding more.

4 When more than half the stock has been absorbed, add the kale, a handful at a time, and stir well to combine. Cook for 20–25 minutes or until the kale has wilted and all the stock has been absorbed. Then stir in the cream and Parmesan.

5 Meanwhile, heat the remaining oil in a small frying pan over medium-high heat. Add the bacon and cook for 7 minutes, until cooked through and starting to crisp up. Remove with a slotted spoon, add to the risotto, and mix well to combine. Season with salt and pepper, sprinkle with Parmesan, and serve hot.

ROASTED VEGETABLE FARRO RISOTTO

This rich and delicious risotto uses farro for its chewy texture and slightly sweet flavor. The addition of roasted vegetables makes this a warm and satisfying meal.

SERVES 4 · PREP 15 MINS · COOK 40 MINS

3 tbsp olive oil

1 small onion, finely chopped

¾ cup uncooked farro

½ cup white wine

1 quart hot chicken stock

½ cup freshly grated Parmesan cheese

1 tbsp finely chopped thyme

sea salt and freshly ground black pepper

1 red bell pepper, seeded and thinly sliced

1 zucchini, diced

5½oz (150g) cherry tomatoes

1 Preheat the oven to 400°F (200°C). Heat 1 tablespoon of the oil in a large saucepan over medium heat. Add the onion and cook for about 5 minutes, stirring frequently, until softened. Then add the farro, stir to mix, and cook on low heat for 1–2 minutes.

2 Stir the wine into the pan and leave to cook until all the liquid has been absorbed. Then add the stock a ladleful at a time, stirring constantly, allowing the liquid to be fully absorbed before adding more. Once all the liquid has been absorbed, add the Parmesan and thyme, and season to taste. Remove from the heat.

3 Meanwhile, arrange the bell peppers, zucchini, and tomatoes on a baking sheet. Drizzle over the remaining oil and season with salt and pepper. Transfer the sheet to the oven and roast the vegetables for 20–25 minutes, stirring occasionally, until cooked through and golden. Stir the roasted vegetables into the risotto and serve immediately.

KAMUT AND FENNEL RISOTTO

Fennel is a member of the celery family and very popular in Mediterranean countries. Kamut has a far nuttier and richer flavor than traditional risotto rice and is the perfect foil for the slight licorice taste of the fresh fennel.

SERVES 2 · PREP 10 MINS, PLUS OVERNIGHT SOAKING · COOK 1 HR

1 cup uncooked kamut, soaked overnight

3 cups chicken or vegetable stock

1 tbsp butter

1 tbsp olive oil

1 fennel bulb, diced and fronds reserved

1 onion, diced

1 garlic clove, crushed

4fl oz (125ml) white wine

1 tsp grated lemon zest

⅓ cup freshly grated Parmesan cheese, plus extra to serve

salt and freshly ground black pepper

1 Place the kamut and stock in a large, lidded saucepan and bring to a boil. Then reduce the heat to a simmer, cover, and cook for about 45 minutes. Remove from the heat. Strain the kamut, reserving any remaining liquid, and set aside.

2 Heat the butter and oil in a large, deep-sided saucepan over medium heat. Add the fennel and onions and cook for about 5 minutes, stirring frequently, until softened. Then add the garlic and cook for another 2 minutes.

3 Add the kamut and wine and cook, stirring frequently, until the wine has been absorbed. Then add about ¼ cup of the reserved stock and cook, stirring frequently, until the liquid is fully absorbed and the kamut is tender but still has some bite. Check the texture of the kamut frequently and add more stock if needed.

4 Add the lemon zest and Parmesan, stir well to combine, and remove from the heat. Season to taste, garnish with fennel fronds, and sprinkle with some Parmesan. Serve immediately.

fennel bulb

CURRIED LENTIL QUINOA PILAF

With all the flavors of an indian curry that are lifted by the fresh ginger, this filling pilaf is packed full of goodness as the quinoa and lentils make a powerful and nutritious combination.

SERVES 4 · PREP 10 MINS · COOK 40 MINS

2 tbsp olive oil

½ onion, finely chopped

2 garlic cloves, crushed

2 tsp grated fresh ginger

1 tbsp garam masala

⅓ cup dried lentils, rinsed

½ cup quinoa

2oz (60g) frozen peas

salt and freshly ground black pepper

1 Heat the oil in a large, lidded saucepan over medium heat. Add the onions and cook for 6–8 minutes, stirring frequently, until translucent. Then add the garlic, ginger, and garam masala, stir to combine, and cook for 1 more minute. Add the lentils and 2 cups of water, stir to mix, and bring to a boil.

2 Reduce the heat to medium-low, cover, and cook for about 10 minutes. Then add the quinoa and peas, stir to combine, and cook for another 20 minutes or until the liquid has been absorbed, the lentils are cooked, and the quinoa is tender. Season to taste and remove from the heat. Serve immediately.

garlic cloves

RED PEPPERS STUFFED WITH ARTICHOKE BARLEY RISOTTO

These lightly roasted red bell peppers are the perfect vessels for a creamy barley risotto dotted with artichoke hearts and are a delightful change from the conventional stuffed peppers.

SERVES 6 · PREP 10 MINS · COOK 35 MINS

¼ cup extra virgin olive oil

1 small onion, diced

1 cup uncooked barley

½ cup white wine

1 quart warm vegetable stock

1 cup freshly grated Parmesan cheese

12oz (350g) artichoke hearts, chopped

salt and freshly ground black pepper

6 red bell peppers

1 Heat 2 tablespoons of the oil in a large saucepan over medium heat. Add the onion and cook, stirring frequently, for 5–10 minutes or until translucent and lightly browned. Then add the barley, stir to mix, and cook for another 1–2 minutes.

2 Stir the wine into the pan and leave to cook until all the liquid had been absorbed. Then add the stock a ladleful at a time, stirring constantly, allowing the liquid to be fully absorbed before adding more. Once all the stock has been added, cook, stirring constantly, for about 2–3 minutes or until all the stock has been absorbed. Remove from the heat, stir in the Parmesan and artichoke hearts, and season to taste.

3 Preheat the oven to 350°F (180°C). Slice the red bell peppers in half lengthwise. Core, seed, and remove the white veins from the inside and discard. Rub the peppers with the remaining oil and place on a baking sheet lined with foil. Roast in the oven for 15 minutes, until softened. Remove from the heat. Divide the risotto mixture into 6 equal parts and use to fill the peppers. Serve immediately.

CHICKEN-FRIED FREEKEH

Based on the popular Chinese dish of egg-fried rice, this easy-to-make recipe uses freekeh instead of rice as a healthy alternative, with the sesame oil and soy sauce providing the traditional tangy elements.

SERVES 4 · PREP 10 MINS · COOK 35 MINS

1 cup cracked freekeh

1 tbsp olive oil

2 large garlic cloves, crushed

2 scallions, thinly sliced

8oz (225g) cooked chicken, diced

1 tsp sesame oil

salt and freshly ground black pepper

2 large eggs, beaten lightly

¼ cup low-sodium soy sauce

1 Rinse the freekeh under running water and drain well. Place in a large saucepan, cover with 1 quart of water, and bring to a boil. Then reduce the heat to a simmer and cook for 15 minutes, until almost all of the water has been absorbed. Remove from the heat and set aside.

2 Heat the olive oil in a wok or large, nonstick frying pan over medium heat. Add the garlic and onions and cook for 3–4 minutes, stirring frequently, until the onions are softened.

3 Add the freekeh and stir to incorporate. Then add the chicken and sesame oil, season with salt and pepper, and mix until well combined. Cook for about 4 minutes, stirring frequently, until the chicken is heated through.

4 Move the freekeh mixture to one side of the pan, making a little space in the other. Pour the eggs in and cook for 2–3 minutes, without stirring, until firm. Then stir well to mix and cook for another 1–2 minutes, until cooked through.

5 Mix the eggs with the freekeh and chicken mixture, scraping up the pan juices, and cook for another 1–2 minutes or until well combined. Remove from the heat, drizzle the soy sauce over it, and mix well. Serve hot.

WHOLESOME BURGERS AND LIGHT MEALS

QUINOA FALAFEL
WITH MINT YOGURT SAUCE

The addition of quinoa to the traditional falafel gives them an added whole grain goodness and a unique flavor and texture. It is paired here with a fresh and light yogurt sauce to complement the earthy spices.

SERVES 4 · PREP 15 MINS, PLUS CHILLING · COOK 45 MINS

⅓ cup uncooked quinoa

1 egg

2 garlic cloves

1 tbsp cumin

¼ tsp salt

2 x 14oz (400g) can chickpeas, drained

¼ cup chopped cilantro leaves

1 tbsp all-purpose flour, for dusting

1–2 tbsp olive oil, plus extra for greasing

FOR THE SAUCE

⅔ cup Greek yogurt

¼ cup chopped mint leaves

juice of 1 lemon

1 Rinse the quinoa under running water, place in a large saucepan, and cover with ⅔ cup of water. Place the pan over medium heat and bring to a simmer. Cook the quinoa for 15 minutes or until almost all the water has been absorbed. Remove from the heat, drain any remaining water, and set aside.

2 Place the quinoa, egg, garlic, cumin, salt, and ½ cup of the chickpeas in a food processor. Pulse until well combined. Add the cilantro and the remaining chickpeas and pulse lightly for 1 minute, until the chickpeas have broken down but still retain some of their texture. Transfer the mixture to a large bowl and chill in the fridge for 30 minutes.

3 Preheat the oven to 400°F (200°C). Grease and line a baking sheet with parchment paper. Divide the falafel mixture into eight equal portions. On a lightly floured surface, roll each portion into a smooth ball and press down lightly to form patty-like shapes.

4 Brush the falafel with a little oil on both sides and place on the baking sheet. Bake in the oven for 20 minutes or until the falafel are well browned and crispy on the outside. Remove from the heat.

5 For the sauce, place all the ingredients in a bowl and mix well. Serve the falafel and mint yogurt sauce with pita breads and a green salad, if liked.

TEFF STACKS
WITH MEDITERRANEAN VEGETABLES

The versatile teff is used here to make tasty fried patties and combined with the classic Mediterranean trio of eggplant, tomato, and mozzarella. Perfect when served on a warm day with crusty bread and a glass of chilled white wine.

SERVES 4 · PREP 20 MINS, PLUS COOLING · COOK 30 MINS

3 cups hot vegetable stock

1 cup uncooked teff

1 eggplant, sliced into 8 x ¼in (5mm) wide rounds

salt and freshly ground black pepper

1 tbsp olive oil, plus extra to serve

2 large tomatoes, sliced into 8 x ¼in (5mm) wide rounds

7oz (200g) mozzarella cheese, sliced into 8 x ¼in (5mm) wide rounds

handful of basil leaves, to garnish

1 Grease and line two 8 x 10in (20 x 25cm) baking sheets with parchment paper and set aside. Place the stock in a large saucepan and bring to a simmer over medium-high heat. Then add the teff and stir well to mix.

2 Reduce the heat to medium and cook for 15–20 minutes, stirring frequently to avoid lumps, until the teff thickens to an oatmeal-like consistency. Remove from the heat. Divide the teff equally between the prepared trays and use a wooden spoon to spread into a smooth and even layer. Set aside to cool and firm up.

3 Place the eggplant slices in a colander, sprinkle with ¼ teaspoon of salt, and set aside to draw out the water. Remove the teff from the baking sheets and place on a clean work surface. Cut out eight large rounds using a cookie cutter or the bottom of a glass.

4 Heat a griddle pan over high heat. Dry the eggplant slices with paper towels and grill on the griddle pan for 2 minutes on each side, until lightly chargrilled and tender. Remove from the heat and set aside.

5 Heat the oil in a large frying pan over medium-high heat. Fry the teff rounds for 2 minutes on each side, until crisp. Set aside. Then fry the tomato slices for 1–2 minutes on each side and remove from the heat.

6 To assemble the stacks, place one teff round on each of four plates. Top each of these with a slice of eggplant, tomato, and mozzarella. Repeat to get two layers of each ingredient. Season with pepper, sprinkle the basil over them, and drizzle with oil. Serve immediately.

CAULIFLOWER HAZELNUT POLENTA

it may seem difficult to skin the hazelnuts, but the skins can be quite bitter and will change the taste of the dish if left on. The sweetness of the roasted nuts contrasts well with the cauliflower and the ripeness of the Manchego.

SERVES 4 · PREP 15 MINS · COOK 45 MINS

½ cup hazelnuts

1lb (450g) cauliflower, cut into florets

1 tbsp olive oil

salt and freshly ground black pepper

juice of half a lemon

FOR THE POLENTA

2½ cups milk, plus extra if needed

1 cup coarse polenta

3 tbsp unsalted butter

⅓ cup Manchego cheese, shredded, plus extra to serve

handful of flat-leaf parsley, coarsely chopped, to garnish

1 Preheat the oven to 350°F (180°C). Spread out the hazelnuts on a baking sheet, place in the oven, and toast for 10–15 minutes or until they are well browned with the skins peeling off. Leave them to cool slightly. Then place them between two pieces of paper towel and rub to remove the skins. Coarsely chop the hazelnuts and set aside.

2 Increase the heat to 400°F (200°C). Place the cauliflower on a large baking sheet, drizzle with the oil, and season well. Place in the oven and roast for 30 minutes, stirring occasionally, until golden brown and cooked through. Remove from the heat, drizzle with the lemon juice, and set aside.

3 For the polenta, place the milk and 2 cups of water in a large, lidded, nonstick saucepan. Add ¼ teaspoon salt and a good grinding of pepper. Bring to a boil, then reduce the heat to medium-low. Gradually add one-third of the polenta, stirring constantly, until well combined. Then add the remaining polenta, stirring constantly, and cook for about 10 minutes or until it is well combined and smooth.

4 Reduce the heat to low and cover partially. Cook for another 15 minutes, stirring occasionally to ensure it does not stick to the bottom, until it is creamy. Add a little more water or milk to the pan if the polenta seems too thick. Then stir in the butter and cheese and mix well to incorporate. Remove from the heat. Spoon the polenta into serving bowls and top with the hazelnuts and cauliflower. Garnish with parsley and serve immediately.

SEEDED BEET AND BUCKWHEAT BURGERS

These hearty and earthy vegetarian burgers combine the sweetness of beet and the nutty texture of seeds with wholesome buckwheat. You won't miss the meat with these!

SERVES 4 · PREP 15 MINS, PLUS SOAKING AND CHILLING · COOK 30 MINS

⅓ cup uncooked buckwheat

4½oz (125g) beets, unpeeled and coarsely chopped

3oz (85g) carrot, unpeeled and coarsely chopped

1oz (30g) scallions, trimmed and finely chopped

2 eggs

⅓ cup oats

½ tsp salt

½ cup sunflower seeds

2–3 tbsp vegetable oil

1 Place the buckwheat in a large bowl and cover with water. Cover the bowl with a dish towel and leave to soak for at least 8 hours or for up to 12 hours. Then drain and rinse under running water.

2 Place the beets, carrots, and onions in a food processor and pulse for 1–2 minutes to combine. Then add the buckwheat, eggs, oats, and salt and pulse until just incorporated.

3 Add all but 1 tablespoon of the sunflower seeds to the mixture, pulse to combine, and transfer to a large bowl. Add the remaining sunflower seeds and stir to combine. Chill in the fridge for 30 minutes. Divide the mixture into 4 equal portions, then shape each portion into a 4in (9cm) wide and ¾in (2cm) thick burger patty.

4 Heat the oil in a nonstick frying pan over medium-high heat. Add the patties, once the oil is hot, and fry for about 5 minutes on each side or until firm and lightly colored. Do this in batches to avoid overcrowding the pan. Remove from the heat and drain on a plate lined with paper towels. Serve with buns, some mayonnaise, fries, and a green salad.

GRAIN EXCHANGE

You could use the same quantity of either of these grains instead of the buckwheat. Soak them in water overnight, then cook in ¾ cup of water, and drain well. Leave to cool before using in the same way as the buckwheat.

quinoa

farro

millet

why not try...

Use **pumpkin seeds** in place of the sunflower seeds.

TEX MEX BURRITOS

An easy-to-make vegetable and millet wrap that makes for a delightful toasty, cheesy dinner.

SERVES 4 · PREP 15 MINS · COOK 20 MINS

1 tbsp olive oil	4 large tortillas
1 garlic clove, crushed	1 cup freshly grated Cheddar cheese
1 jalapeño pepper, finely chopped	1 avocado, pitted and sliced
¼ cup lime juice	½ cup salsa (see p43)
1 cup prepared millet (see p22)	
7oz (200g) can black beans	

1 Preheat the oven to 375°F (190°C). Heat the oil in a frying pan over medium heat. Add the garlic and jalapeños and cook for 2 minutes, stirring occasionally, until the garlic is softened.

2 Then stir in the lime juice, millet, and black beans. Mix to combine and cook for 7 minutes or until heated through. Remove from the heat.

3 Divide the mixture evenly between the tortillas and top with equal quantities of the cheese, avocado, and salsa. Wrap the tortillas over the filling to form burritos. Enclose each burrito in a sheet of foil and cook in the oven for 10 minutes. Serve immediately.

BULGUR WHEAT, CARROT, AND ZUCCHINI FRITTERS

These are great as a quick snack, or to accompany roasted chicken or a burger.

SERVES 4 · PREP 10 MINS, PLUS COOLING · COOK 40 MINS

⅓ cup uncooked bulgur wheat	4 large eggs, lightly beaten
1 zucchini, grated	salt and freshly ground black pepper
1 carrot, grated	2 tbsp light olive oil
1 tbsp coarsely chopped flat-leaf parsley	

1 Place the bulgur wheat in a pan, cover with 1¼ cups of water, and bring to a boil. Then reduce the heat to a simmer and cook for 20–30 minutes or until all the water has been absorbed and the bulgur wheat is soft. Remove from the heat and leave to cool for 15 minutes.

2 Place all the vegetables in a clean dish towel and squeeze out as much water as possible. Then transfer to a bowl and add the parsley, bulgur wheat, and eggs. Season with salt and pepper and mix well to combine.

3 Heat the oil in a large, nonstick frying pan over medium-high heat. Add heaped spoonfuls of the vegetable mixture and lightly spread them out so that each fritter is about 3in (7.5cm) in diameter and ½in (1cm) thick. Fry the fritters for 2–3 minutes on each side, until golden brown on the outside and cooked through. Do this in batches to avoid overcrowding the pan. Remove with a slotted spoon and place on a lined plate. Serve hot.

FREEKEH KOFTE
WITH A TAHINI LEMON SAUCE

Traditionally made with ground beef or lamb, these meatballs are very popular in the Middle East and across Asia. The use of freekeh turns this version of kofte into a perfect vegetarian meal.

SERVES 4 · PREP 15 MINS, PLUS COOLING AND CHILLING · COOK 45 MINS

1 cup cracked freekeh

1 small onion, finely chopped

1 egg

2 tsp ground cumin

1 tsp ground coriander

3 tbsp coarsely chopped mint

3 tbsp coarsely chopped
flat-leaf parsley

½ tsp salt

2 tbsp oats

⅓ cup whole wheat flour, plus
extra if needed

¼ cup olive oil

FOR THE SAUCE

¼ cup tahini sesame paste

juice of 1 lemon

1 garlic clove, finely chopped

¼ tsp salt

2 tbsp coarsely chopped
flat-leaf parsley

1 Place the freekeh and 1 quart of water in a large, lidded saucepan. Bring to a boil, then reduce the heat to a simmer. Cook for 20 minutes or until all the water has been absorbed and the freekeh is thick and sticky in texture. Remove from the heat, drain any remaining water, and leave to cool.

2 Add the onions, egg, cumin, coriander, mint, parsley, salt, oats, and flour to the freekeh. Mix well to combine and place in the fridge to chill for at least 30 minutes.

3 Meanwhile, for the sauce, place the tahini, lemon juice, garlic, salt, and parsley in a bowl. Add ¼ cup of water and mix well to make a smooth paste. Add more water if the sauce seems too thick. Set aside.

4 On a clean work surface, shape the freekeh mixture into small balls about 1½in (4cm) in diameter. Add more flour if the mixture seems too loose and is not sticking together.

5 Heat 2 tablespoons of the oil in a nonstick frying pan over medium-high heat. Once the oil is hot, add the kofte to the pan and fry for 5–8 minutes, turning frequently, until well browned all over and crispy on the outside. Remove with a slotted spoon, place on a lined plate, and keep warm. Do this in batches to avoid overcrowding the pan. Serve hot with the tahini sauce.

lemons

AMARANTH BLACK BEAN BURGERS
WITH AVOCADO CREAM

These vegetarian burgers are more than a match for any meat alternative. With a great texture from the combination of black beans and chewy amaranth and a hint of chile, they work perfectly with the cool avocado cream.

SERVES 6 · PREP 15 MINS, PLUS COOLING · COOK 45 MINS

⅓ cup uncooked amaranth

14oz (400g) can black beans, drained

1 small red onion, finely chopped

½ tsp garlic granules, or ¼ tsp garlic powder

½ tsp chile flakes

1 tbsp oats

¼ tsp salt

6 burger buns, to serve

handful of cherry tomatoes, thinly sliced

1 small red onion, sliced into rings

FOR THE AVOCADO CREAM

2 avocados

juice of 1 lemon

pinch of salt

1 Place the amaranth in a large saucepan and cover with ½ cup of water. Bring to a boil, then reduce to a simmer, and cook for 12 minutes or until all the water has been absorbed. Remove from the heat, drain any remaining water, and leave to cool slightly.

2 Preheat the oven to 400°F (200°C). Grease and line a baking sheet with parchment paper. Transfer the amaranth to a large bowl. Add the beans, onions, garlic granules, and chile flakes. Mix well, using the back of a fork to mash the ingredients together. Then add the oats and salt to the mixture. Mix until well incorporated.

3 Divide the mixture into 6 equal portions and shape each into a ball. Gently press down each ball to form a burger patty about 3in (7.5cm) in diameter. Place the patties on the prepared baking sheet and transfer to the oven. Bake for 30 minutes or until they are firm to the touch and crispy on the outside.

4 For the avocado cream, scoop out the flesh from the avocado and place in a food processor. Add the lemon juice and salt and pulse until smooth. Place the burgers in the buns and top with the avocado cream. Serve alongside the tomatoes and onions.

BEEF AND BARLEY BURGERS

Burgers, but with a whole grain upgrade. Adding the cooked barley makes these burgers tender and moist with a great texture. ideal for your next barbecue!

MAKES 4 LARGE BURGERS · PREP 20 MINS, PLUS COOLING AND CHILLING · COOK 1 HR

¼ cup uncooked pearl barley

1lb 2oz (500g) lean ground beef

1 large egg

3½oz (100g) onions, finely chopped

1 tsp mixed dried Italian herbs

salt and freshly ground black pepper

1 tbsp olive oil, plus extra for greasing

1 Rinse the barley under cold running water, drain, and place in a large saucepan. Cover with water and bring to a simmer. Cook the barley for 30 minutes or until tender. Then drain, rinse under running water, and drain well again. Set aside to cool.

2 Place the beef, egg, onions, and herbs in a large bowl. Season with salt and pepper and mix well to combine. Add the cooled barley to the bowl and mix until evenly incorporated.

3 Lightly grease a plate. Form the mixture into 4 patties, each roughly 4in (10cm) in diameter and ¾in (2cm) thick. Place them on the greased plate and cover with plastic wrap. Chill the patties for about 20 minutes to help them keep their shape on cooking.

4 Heat the oil in a large frying pan over medium heat. Cook the burger patties for about 10 minutes on each side, until well browned and cooked through. Remove from the heat. Serve the burgers with a selection of buns and accompaniments.

GRAiN EXCHANGE

For a variation, try using the same amount of either of these grains instead of the barley and cook them in the same way.

spelt

farro

VEGGIE BURGER WITH SPELT

These vegetarian burgers get their intense flavor from the super-absorbent spelt. Roasting the vegetables before they are added to the burgers helps retain more of their flavor and keeps the unnecessary moisture out.

MAKES 6 PATTIES · PREP 15 MINS, PLUS OVERNIGHT SOAKING AND CHILLING · COOK 1 HR

¼ cup uncooked spelt

5oz (140g) shiitake mushrooms, sliced

3 tsp tamari or low-sodium soy sauce

1 large beet, about 3½oz (100g), grated

2 large carrots, about 3½oz (100g), grated

14oz (400g) can kidney beans, drained

salt and freshly ground black pepper

1–2 tbsp olive oil

½ cup ground almonds

⅓ cup panko bread crumbs

2 tbsp spicy Dijon mustard

2 tbsp mayonnaise

2 scallions, sliced

2 garlic cloves, pressed

2 large eggs

4oz (115g) tempeh, crumbled

FOR SERVING

6 burger buns

1 avocado, pitted and sliced

1 large tomato, sliced into rounds

1 large red onion, sliced into rounds

1 Place the spelt in a bowl, cover with water, and leave to soak overnight. Then drain well and rinse under running water. Place the spelt in a lidded saucepan. Pour in 1 cup of water and bring to a boil. Then reduce the heat to a simmer, cover, and cook for 50 minutes. Remove from the heat and set aside to cool.

2 Preheat the oven to 425°F (220°C). Spread out the mushrooms on a lined baking sheet and toss with 2 teaspoons of the tamari sauce. Spread out the beets, carrots, and beans on a separate sheet. Season with salt and pepper and toss with the oil. Place the sheets in the oven and bake for 15 minutes. Then remove from the heat and lightly toss the vegetables and mushrooms. Return to the oven, rotating the positions of the sheets. Bake for another 10 minutes or until the vegetables and beans are crisp and the mushrooms have lost most of their moisture. Remove from the heat and leave to cool.

3 Place the ground almonds, bread crumbs, cooled vegetables, and remaining tamari in a food processor and pulse until just combined. Add the mustard, mayonnaise, scallions, garlic, and eggs to the mixture. Season to taste with pepper and pulse to combine. Then add the spelt and tempeh and pulse lightly until just mixed, but still retaining some texture. Transfer the mixture to a large bowl, cover, and chill in the fridge for about 1 hour.

4 Set the broiler or griddle pan at its medium-low setting. Divide the mixture into 6 equal portions and form them into 1in (2.5cm) thick patties. Broil the patties for about 5 minutes on each side, until crisp on the outside. Remove from the heat. Serve hot with burger buns, avocado, tomatoes, and onions.

QUINOA SALMON CAKES

A fresh take on fish cakes, the peppers and quinoa add a whole new dimension to this quick recipe. Serve these easy-to-make cakes with a light tossed salad for a delicious and filling meal.

SERVES 4 · PREP 10 MINS, PLUS CHILLING · COOK 20 MINS

14¾oz (418g) can salmon, drained, flaked, and pin boned

½ cup prepared quinoa (see p22)

2 eggs, beaten

2 garlic cloves, crushed

grated zest of 1 lemon

1½oz (40g) green bell peppers, seeded and finely chopped

1 tsp freshly ground black pepper

sea salt

2–3 tbsp olive oil

1 lemon, cut into wedges, to serve

1 Place the salmon, quinoa, eggs, garlic, lemon zest, green bell peppers, and black pepper in a large bowl. Season to taste with sea salt and mix well until fully incorporated.

2 Divide the mixture into eight equal-sized portions. Gently form each portion into a patty-like shape. Place the cakes on a plate and chill in the fridge for about 15 minutes.

3 Heat the oil in a large frying pan over medium heat. Gently place the cakes in the pan and fry for 4 minutes on each side, until golden brown and cooked through. Do this in batches to avoid overcrowding the pan. Remove from the heat and serve hot with lemon wedges and a watercress salad.

GRAIN EXCHANGE

For a change, try replacing the quinoa with the same amount of prepared **millet** and cook in the same way.

why not try...

For a variation, add cooked **white crab meat** or **tuna** instead of the salmon and cook as given in the recipe.

LAMB AND TEFF MEATBALLS

These impressive meatballs are moist and full of flavor, due to the inclusion of cinnamon, nutmeg, and teff.

SERVES 4 · PREP 10 MINS, PLUS CHILLING · COOK 20 MINS

⅓ cup teff flour	¼ tsp grated nutmeg
1lb (450g) ground lamb	¼ tsp ground cinnamon
2 scallions, about 1oz (30g) in total, finely diced	salt and freshly ground black pepper
1 tsp ground cumin	1 egg, lightly beaten

1 Place the flour, lamb, onions, cumin, nutmeg, and cinnamon in a large bowl. Season with ½ teaspoon of salt and a good grinding of pepper. Mix well to combine. Then add the egg and mix until fully incorporated. Cover the bowl with plastic wrap and place in the fridge for 30 minutes.

2 Preheat the oven to 350°F (180°C). Line a baking sheet with parchment paper. Divide the mixture into 12 equal portions and shape into balls. Place the meatballs on the baking sheet and bake in the oven for 10 minutes.

3 Remove from the heat and turn the meatballs over. Return to the oven and bake for another 10 minutes. Remove from the oven and check the meatballs for doneness. They will be cooked to medium. If you prefer them well done, return the meatballs to the oven for an additional 5 minutes. Remove from the heat and serve warm.

CHIPOTLE BLACK BEAN BURGERS

This quick and easy recipe combines whole grains and spicy chipotle chiles to make the perfect burger patties.

MAKES 6 · PREP 10 MINS · COOK 20 MINS

14oz (400g) can black beans, drained and rinsed	1¼ cups prepared bulgur wheat (see p22)
1 small onion, quartered	½ cup oats
2 cloves garlic	1 large egg
2 chipotle peppers in 1 tsp adobo sauce	½ avocado, pitted and thinly sliced
½ tsp salt	1 large tomato, sliced into rounds

1 Preheat the oven to 375°F (190°C). Place the black beans, onions, garlic, chipotle peppers, and adobo sauce in a food processor. Pulse until well combined. Transfer the mixture to a bowl.

2 Lightly grease a baking sheet and set aside. Add the salt, bulgur wheat, oats, and egg to the bowl. Mix well until evenly combined. Divide the mixture into six equal portions and form each into a burger patty. Place the patties in the baking sheet and place in the oven.

3 Bake for 10–12 minutes, then remove from the oven. Turn the patties over and return to the oven for another 10 minutes, until browned and cooked through. Remove from the heat. Serve immediately with buns and avocado, tomatoes, and lettuce.

BAKED FREEKEH ARANCINI

Arancini balls are typically made from leftover risotto. This recipe recreates this tasty italian treat with freekeh and a unique mozzarella and pine nut filling for a healthier and nuttier dish.

MAKES 12 · PREP 15 MINS, PLUS CHILLING · COOK 50 MINS

1 cup cracked freekeh

2½ cups chicken stock

⅓ cup freshly grated
  mozzarella cheese

2 tbsp pine nuts, lightly
  toasted and finely chopped

1 tbsp finely chopped
  flat-leaf parsley

salt and freshly ground
  black pepper

2 large eggs, lightly beaten

⅓ cup freshly grated
  Parmesan cheese

¾ cup panko bread crumbs

2 tbsp canola oil

marinara sauce, to serve

1 Place the freekeh and stock in a large saucepan and bring to a boil. Reduce the heat to a simmer and cook for 25 minutes. Remove from the heat and drain any remaining water. Spread out the freekeh on a large plate and leave to cool completely. Then place in the fridge to chill.

2 Preheat the oven to 425°F (220°C). Line a baking sheet with parchment paper and set aside. Place the mozzarella, pine nuts, and parsley in a bowl. Add a pinch of salt, season to taste with pepper, and mix well to combine. In a separate bowl, place the eggs, Parmesan, and ½ cup of the bread crumbs. Add the freekeh and mix well to combine. Place the remaining bread crumbs in a shallow dish.

3 Divide the freekeh mixture into 12 equal parts and form into balls. Use your finger to press through the middle of each ball, to form a hole. Fill these with the mozzarella mixture and pinch the sides together to seal. Brush the balls with the oil, then lightly toss through the bread crumbs to coat.

4 Place the balls on the prepared baking sheet, transfer to the oven, and bake for 20–25 minutes, until golden brown. Then remove from the heat and serve warm with marinara sauce. These can be stored for up to 1 day in the fridge.

POLENTA WITH TOMATO, MOZZARELLA, PROSCIUTTO, AND PESTO

As a healthy alternative to fried bread, polenta is the perfect foundation for this light lunch or dinner dish. The salty Prosciutto is complemented by the creamy mozzarella, with the pesto adding a hint of warm italian summers.

SERVES 4 · PREP 15 MINS · COOK 10 MINS

1 tbsp light olive oil

8 x ½in (1cm) thick slices of baked polenta (see p25) or precooked, store-bought polenta, about 10oz (300g) in total

2 tomatoes, cut into 8 slices

8 x ½in (1cm) thick slices of mozzarella cheese, about 10oz (300g) in total

8 slices of prosciutto

3oz (85g) store-bought basil pesto (or see p63 for step-by-step instructions)

1 Heat the oil in a large frying pan set over medium heat. Add the polenta and fry for about 5 minutes on each side, until golden brown. Remove from the pan.

2 Divide the polenta slices between four plates. Top each one with a slice of tomato and mozzarella. Place a slice of prosciutto on each stack and drizzle evenly with the pesto. Serve immediately.

basil

BEEF AND BULGUR WHEAT MEATBALLS
WITH CREAMY PESTO SAUCE

This dish brings together flavorsome and wholesome meatballs with a delightful sauce made from traditional pesto mixed with whipping cream. It's the perfect recipe for a delicious dinner.

SERVES 4 · PREP 10 MINS · COOK 35 MINS

1lb (450g) ground beef

½ cup fresh bread crumbs, seasoned with salt and pepper

⅓ cup prepared bulgur wheat (see p22)

2 large eggs

1 tbsp pesto (see p63)

½ tsp salt

¼ tsp pepper

FOR THE SAUCE

1 tbsp butter

1 tbsp all-purpose flour

1 cup heavy cream

8oz (225g) pesto

1 Preheat the oven to 375°F (190°C). Lightly grease a baking sheet and set aside. Place the beef, bread crumbs, bulgur wheat, eggs, and pesto in a large bowl. Season with the salt and pepper. Mix until thoroughly combined.

2 Form the mixture into 12 balls and arrange on the prepared baking sheet. Bake the meatballs for 15 minutes, then remove from the oven and flip them over. Return the meatballs to the oven and bake for another 10 minutes, until cooked through.

3 Meanwhile, for the sauce, melt the butter in a saucepan. Add the flour and cook, whisking constantly, until it turns a pale golden color. Then add the cream, a little at a time, and whisk constantly until fully incorporated.

4 Add the pesto and whisk until thoroughly combined. Season to taste if needed, and mix well to combine. Serve the meatballs hot with the sauce poured over them.

BAKED BUTTERNUT SQUASH FRiTTERS

These appealing and healthy fritters are baked instead of fried. The amaranth flour brings a slightly nutty note to the dish and the polenta adds the crispness usually attained from deep-frying.

MAKES 10 FRiTTERS · PREP 15 MiNS, PLUS COOLING · COOK 1 HR 15 MiNS

1 small butternut squash, about 10oz (300g)

⅓ cup amaranth flour

1 garlic clove, pressed

2 tbsp coarsely chopped chives

½ tsp ground cumin

¼ tsp cayenne pepper

salt and freshly ground black pepper

1 tbsp extra virgin olive oil

1 tbsp maple syrup

½ cup freshly grated Parmesan cheese

½ cup polenta

1 Preheat the oven to 400°F (200°C). Use a fork to poke holes in the butternut squash, then place it in a roasting pan. Place the pan in the oven and roast for about 45 minutes, until soft. Remove from the heat and leave to cool slightly. Reduce the temperature to 350°F (180°C). Line a baking sheet with parchment paper and set aside.

2 Once cooled, cut the squash in half and remove the seeds. Scoop out all the flesh and place in a large bowl. Use the back of a fork to mash the squash until smooth. Then add the amaranth, garlic, chives, cumin, and cayenne pepper. Season with a pinch of salt and a good grinding of black pepper. Stir to combine. Pour in the oil and maple syrup. Sprinkle in the cheese and mix well to combine.

3 Place the polenta in a shallow dish. Take spoonfuls of the squash mixture, form into balls, and toss in the polenta to coat. Lay the balls on the prepared baking sheet and flatten slightly. Bake the fritters for 25–30 minutes or until golden brown and cooked through. Serve warm.

chives

SAUSAGE AND FARRO STUFFED PORTABELLA MUSHROOMS

Mild sausages are combined with earthy farro and roasted mushrooms in this wonderfully textured dish. Serve them on their own as an appetizer or pair with a tossed salad for a light dinner.

SERVES 4 · PREP 15 MiNS · COOK 40 MiNS

5½oz (150g) sweet Italian sausages

1 tbsp olive oil

1 small onion, finely diced

1 green bell pepper, seeded and finely diced

4 large portabella mushroom caps, stems reserved and finely chopped

½ cup prepared farro (see p22)

1 large egg, lightly beaten

1 tsp smoked paprika

salt and freshly ground black pepper

1 Preheat the oven to 375°F (190°C). Heat a small frying pan over medium heat. Add the sausages and cook for 5–10 minutes or until well browned and cooked through. Remove from the heat and leave to cool slightly before chopping into bite-sized pieces.

2 Heat the oil in a frying pan over medium heat. Add the onions, green bell peppers, and mushroom stems. Cook for about 10 minutes, stirring occasionally, until lightly browned. Transfer to a large bowl, add the sausages and farro, and mix to combine. Then add the egg and smoked paprika and season to taste. Stir well to combine.

3 Use a spoon to scrape out and discard the ribs from the mushroom caps. Divide the sausage and farro mixture evenly between the mushroom caps and press down lightly to set. Place on a baking sheet and bake for about 20 minutes or until the caps have softened and the filling has cooked through. Remove from the oven and leave to cool slightly. Serve warm.

POLENTA FRiES WiTH ROSEMARY AND GARLiC

Far healthier than anything served by fast food chains, these polenta fries are boosted in flavor thanks to the rosemary and garlic. Pair them with a spelt veggie burger for the perfect whole grain meal.

SERVES 4–6 · PREP 15 MiNS, PLUS CHiLLiNG · COOK 30 MiNS

1–2 tbsp olive oil, plus extra for greasing

3 cups chicken stock

1 tbsp butter

1 cup quick-cook polenta

1 garlic clove, pressed

1 tbsp finely chopped rosemary

salt and freshly ground black pepper

1 Grease a baking sheet and set aside. Place the stock and butter in a saucepan and bring to a boil. Then reduce the heat to medium-low and gradually add the polenta, whisking constantly. Cook for about 2 minutes, whisking constantly, until all the liquid has been absorbed and the polenta has thickened and is smooth.

2 Remove from the heat, add the garlic and rosemary, and mix well to combine. Transfer the polenta mixture to the baking sheet and spread it out to form an even ½in (1cm) thick layer. Place the baking sheet in the refrigerator to chill for 3 hours.

3 Preheat the oven to 400°F (200°C). Grease another baking sheet and set aside. Place the polenta on a clean surface and slice into long rectangular pieces. Spread out the fries on the prepared baking sheet and lightly brush with oil. Season well and bake for 20–25 minutes or until they are golden brown at the edges. Remove from the heat and serve immediately.

SPICY QUINOA AND KAMUT CAKES
WITH A MANGO HABANERO SAUCE

These tasty and versatile cakes can be served as fun appetizers or finger food and will tingle the taste-buds with their deceptive spiciness. Dip them in the mango habanero sauce for a fiery yet fruity flavor.

MAKES 12 SMALL CAKES · PREP 20 MINS, PLUS OVERNIGHT SOAKING AND CHILLING · COOK 1 HR 10 MINS

½ cup uncooked kamut, soaked overnight

salt and freshly ground black pepper

½ cup uncooked quinoa

3 eggs, lightly beaten

½ cup mustard greens, finely chopped

handful of cilantro, finely chopped

1 jalapeño, seeded and finely chopped

3 shallots, finely chopped

3 garlic cloves, pressed

1 tsp ground cumin

½ tsp baking powder

½ cup chickpea flour

2–4 tbsp canola oil, plus extra if needed

FOR THE SAUCE

1 tbsp canola oil

1 large, ripe mango, pitted and diced

1 small habanero chile, seeded and diced

1 garlic clove, crushed

1 shallot, coarsely chopped

2 tbsp white wine vinegar

1 Place the kamut in a saucepan and cover with 1½ cups of water. Add a pinch of salt and bring to a boil. Then reduce the heat to a simmer, cover, and cook for about 40 minutes. Then remove from the heat, drain any remaining water, and spread out on a baking sheet to cool.

2 Meanwhile, place the quinoa in a separate saucepan and cover with 1 cup of water. Add a pinch of salt and bring to a boil. Then reduce the heat to a simmer, cover, and cook for 10–15 minutes or until almost all the water has been absorbed. Then remove from the heat and drain any remaining water. Transfer to the baking sheet with the kamut and leave to cool to room temperature, then chill in the fridge for 10–15 minutes.

3 For the sauce, heat the oil in a frying pan over medium heat. Add the mango, habanero chile, garlic, shallots, and vinegar. Cook for 10 minutes, stirring frequently, until the mango has softened and broken down. Transfer the mixture to a food processor and pulse until smooth. Place the sauce in a bowl and set aside to cool.

4 Preheat the oven to 350°F (180°C). Place the kamut, quinoa, eggs, mustard greens, cilantro, jalapeños, shallots, garlic, and cumin in a large bowl. Season with ½ teaspoon of salt and a good grinding of pepper and mix well to combine. Then add the baking powder and flour and mix until well combined. Chill in the fridge for 20–25 minutes.

5 Line a baking sheet with parchment paper. Divide the mixture into 12 equal portions and form each one into a ball. Flatten the balls slightly to make patties that are about 2in (5cm) in diameter. Place the patties on the prepared baking sheet. Bake for about 10 minutes. Remove from the heat.

6 Heat the oil in a frying pan over medium heat. Once the oil is hot, place the cakes in the pan and cook for 2–3 minutes on each side, until browned. Do this in batches to avoid overcrowding the pan. Remove from the heat and serve warm with the sauce.

HEARTY STEWS AND BAKED DISHES

KITCHARI STEW WITH KAMUT

The word "kitchari" literally means mixture, and is an Indian recipe that mixes two or more grains for a soothing and warming dish. This recipe uses kamut instead of rice for more texture and bite.

SERVES 3 · PREP 10 MINS, PLUS OVERNIGHT SOAKING · COOK 2 HRS 10 MINS

¾ cup yellow split peas

½ cup uncooked kamut

1 tbsp coconut oil

2in (5cm) piece of fresh ginger, finely chopped

2 tsp turmeric

2 tsp ground cumin

1 tsp ground coriander

½ tsp ground cinnamon

salt

handful of cilantro, to garnish

1 Place the peas in a large bowl, cover with water, and leave to soak for about 12 hours. Place the kamut in a separate bowl, cover with water, and leave to soak overnight or for up to 8 hours. Drain any remaining water from the peas and kamut. Rinse under running water, drain well, and set aside.

2 Heat the oil in a large, lidded saucepan over medium heat. Add the ginger, turmeric, cumin, coriander, and cinnamon. Reduce the heat to low and cook for 1–2 minutes, stirring frequently, making sure the spices do not burn.

3 Add the peas, kamut, and 1½ quarts of water to the pan. Season with salt and bring the mixture to a simmer. Cover partially and cook, stirring occasionally, for 2 hours or until the peas have broken down and the kamut is tender and chewy. Taste and adjust seasoning, if needed. Remove from the heat and garnish with cilantro. Serve hot.

GRAIN EXCHANGE

For a change, use the same amount of either of the following grains in place of the kamut and see p16–17 for advice on cooking times.

spelt

wheat berries

BAKED MOROCCAN LAMB STEW WiTH FREEKEH

Easy to prepare, slow cooking this dish in the oven brings about a warming combination of tenderness from the lamb and a rich and creamy texture from the freekeh. The dried fruit adds something special to every bite.

SERVES 2–3 · PREP 10 MiNS · COOK 2 HRS

1 tbsp olive oil

12oz (350g) boneless lamb shoulder, diced

½ cup uncooked freekeh

14oz (400g) can chopped tomatoes

2 tbsp ground cumin

¼ tsp grated fresh ginger

½ tsp ground cinnamon

¼ tsp salt

¾ cup dried apricots, coarsely chopped

3 tbsp chopped cilantro

1 Preheat the oven to 350°F (180°C). Heat the oil in a large, lidded heatproof dish over medium heat. Add the lamb and cook for about 5 minutes, stirring occasionally, until lightly browned all over. Remove from the heat.

2 Add the freekeh, tomatoes, cumin, ginger, cinnamon, and salt to the lamb and stir well. Then add 1 cup of water and mix to combine. Cover, transfer to the oven, and bake for about 45 minutes.

3 Remove from the oven. Add the apricots to the dish, stir well, and return to the oven. Cook for another hour or until the freekeh is tender and chewy and the lamb is cooked through. Remove from the heat and transfer to a large serving dish. Garnish with cilantro and serve hot.

GRAiN EXCHANGE

This dish works really well with quinoa and millet, too. Use the same amount of grain as the freekeh, reduce the water quantity to ¾ cup for both grains, and cook as above.

quinoa

millet

SHORT RiB STEW OVER POLENTA

A great comfort food for a cold day, this stew is served over polenta, which adds a little more richness to this dish. The braised ribs are deliciously tender and will fill your home with the most wonderful aromas.

SERVES 4–6 · PREP 10 MiNS · COOK 3 HRS 25 MiNS

2 tbsp all-purpose flour

salt and freshly ground black pepper

3lb (1.35kg) boneless short ribs

3 tbsp vegetable oil

16fl oz (500ml) good-quality red wine, such as Cabernet

2½ cups beef stock

1 onion, diced

3 garlic cloves, crushed and sliced, plus 1 garlic clove crushed

4 carrots, diced

3 red potatoes, diced

2½oz (70g) chestnut or baby portobella mushrooms, sliced

1 tsp dried thyme

½ tsp dried rosemary

½ tsp dried sage

2 cups milk

1 cup quick-cook polenta

handful of fresh thyme sprigs, to garnish

handful of watercress, to garnish

1 Place the flour in a shallow dish. Season the short ribs and toss in the flour to coat. Heat the oil in a Dutch oven or large casserole, over medium-high heat. Add the short ribs and cook for 5–6 minutes, until lightly colored on all sides. Then add the wine and bring to a boil. Cook for about 10 minutes or until the liquid has been reduced by half.

2 Add the stock and bring to a boil. Then reduce the heat to low, cover, and simmer for 2–2 ½ hours or until the meat is tender. Check the stew occasionally and skim away any fat from the surface.

3 Add the onions, garlic, carrots, potatoes, and mushrooms and stir to mix. Then add the thyme, rosemary, and sage. Season with ½ teaspoon of salt and pepper. Cook the stew for another 40 minutes until the vegetables are soft and cooked through.

4 Meanwhile, place the milk in a saucepan and season with pepper and ¼ teaspoon of salt. Add 1 cup of water and bring to a boil. Add the polenta, a little at a time, stirring constantly. Reduce the heat to low and cook for 2 minutes, stirring constantly, until the polenta is thick and pulling away from the sides. Add the garlic, season to taste, and mix well. Spoon the polenta into bowls, ladle the stew over it, and garnish with thyme and watercress. Serve hot.

RATATOUiLLE CASSEROLE WiTH FARRO AND FETA

A mix of baked Mediterranean vegetables, tomato sauce, and tender farro is topped with contrasting salty feta cheese for a warm and filling meal that is perfect at any time of the year.

SERVES 4 · PREP 10 MiNS, PLUS OVERNiGHT SOAKiNG · COOK 1 HR 30 MiNS

½ cup uncooked farro

1 eggplant, cut into cubes

½ tsp salt

2 red or orange bell peppers, seeded and cut into bite-sized pieces

1 zucchini, cut into bite-sized pieces

1 red onion, finely chopped

1 tbsp olive oil

14oz (400g) can chopped tomatoes

1 cup vegetable stock

¼ tsp dried rosemary

1 garlic clove, finely chopped

7oz (200g) feta cheese, crumbled

2 tsp chopped basil leaves, to serve

1 Place the farro in a large bowl, cover with water, and leave to soak overnight or for up to 8 hours. Then drain any remaining water, rinse under running water, and drain well again. Set aside.

2 Preheat the oven to 350°F (180°C). Place the eggplant cubes in a colander, sprinkle with the salt, and press down with a heavy object. Leave to draw out the water and any bitterness.

3 Place the bell peppers, zucchini, onions, and eggplant in a 2 quart casserole dish. Spread them out evenly and drizzle with the oil. Add the farro to the dish and toss lightly to mix with the vegetables.

4 Place the tomatoes, stock, rosemary, and garlic in a large bowl and mix to combine. Add the mixture to the casserole dish and mix well. Cover, place in the oven, and bake for 1 hour and 15 minutes or until the vegetables are tender and the farro is cooked.

5 Remove from the heat, take off the lid, and sprinkle over the feta. Return to the oven, uncovered, and cook for about 15 minutes or until the feta starts to turn golden. Remove from the heat and season to taste if needed. Garnish with basil and serve hot.

BEEF AND SPELT STEW

This dish is ideal for when you just want to leave something to cook in the oven while you are busy with other things. Adding spelt to this traditional beef stew provides an extra nutty and chewy texture.

SERVES 4 · PREP 15 MINS, PLUS OVERNIGHT SOAKING · COOK 2 HRS 45 MINS

¾ cup uncooked spelt

2 tbsp olive oil

1 onion, finely chopped

2 celery ribs, finely chopped

2 garlic cloves, finely chopped

1lb 2oz (500g) stew beef, diced

2 carrots, chopped into bite-sized pieces

5½oz (150g) mushrooms, sliced

14oz (400g) can chopped tomatoes

3 cups beef stock

1 tsp dried sage

1 tsp dried thyme

salt and freshly ground black pepper

1 Place the spelt in a bowl, cover with plenty of water, and leave to soak overnight or for up to 8 hours. Then drain and rinse under running cold water. Drain well again and set aside.

2 Preheat the oven to 320°F (160°C). Heat the oil in a frying pan over medium-high heat. Add the onions, celery, and garlic and sauté for about 3 minutes. Then add the beef and cook for 8–10 minutes, stirring frequently, until well browned all over. Remove from the heat.

3 Transfer the beef and onion mixture, along with any juices, to a 3 quart heavy-bottomed ovenproof casserole. Then add the carrots, mushrooms, tomatoes, stock, dried herbs, and spelt. Mix well to combine, cover, and place in the oven.

4 Cook the stew for 2½ hours or until the beef is cooked through and the vegetables and spelt are tender. Remove from the heat. Taste, adjusting the seasoning if needed, and serve hot.

carrots

BAKED CHICKEN FREEKEH PAELLA

This easy one-pot dish works as a simple weekday dinner and is impressive enough to serve when entertaining, too.

SERVES 4 · PREP 15 MINS · COOK 45 MINS

4 chicken legs, about 3lb (1.35kg) in total

salt and freshly ground black pepper

¼ tsp smoked paprika

¼ tsp chile flakes

1⅓ cups uncooked freekeh

1⅔ cups chicken stock

4fl oz (120ml) dry white wine

6oz (175g) chorizo

2 red bell peppers, seeded and thinly sliced

1 red chile, seeded and thinly sliced

1 onion, thinly sliced

5 garlic cloves, smashed and sliced

juice of ½ a lemon

1 tbsp coarsely chopped flat-leaf parsley, to garnish

1 Preheat the oven to 375°F (190°C). Place the chicken legs, skin-side up, on a clean work surface and season generously with salt and pepper. Then rub evenly with the smoked paprika and chile flakes.

2 Place the freekeh, stock, and wine in a large ovenproof casserole. Then add the chorizo, red bell peppers, red chiles, onions, and garlic and place the chicken on top. Cover and transfer the casserole to the oven.

3 Roast for 35 minutes. Then remove the lid and roast for another 10 minutes, until the chicken is cooked through and golden, the freekeh is fluffy, and almost all the liquid has been absorbed. Remove from the heat and drizzle with the lemon juice. Garnish with the parsley and serve hot.

CHEESY CHICKEN AND BROCCOLI CASSEROLE WITH BULGUR WHEAT

Chicken and a creamy cheese sauce combine with bulgur wheat for a comforting casserole.

SERVES 4 · PREP 20 MINS, PLUS COOLING · COOK 30 MINS

3 tbsp unsalted butter

2 tbsp all-purpose flour

3 cups milk

2 tsp mustard powder

salt and freshly ground black pepper

2 cups grated sharp Cheddar cheese

1 cup prepared bulgur wheat (see p22)

8oz (225g) cooked chicken breast, diced

1 small broccoli, cut into florets and steamed

½ cup smoked Gouda cheese, shredded

1 Preheat the oven to 375°F (190°C). Melt the butter in a saucepan over medium heat. Whisk in the flour and cook for about 3 minutes or until golden. Then add the milk and whisk until well combined. Bring to a boil and simmer, whisking constantly, for 5 minutes or until slightly thickened.

2 Remove from the heat and add the mustard. Season to taste and mix well to combine. Add the Cheddar, a little at a time, whisking until fully melted and incorporated. Then add the bulgur wheat, chicken, and broccoli. Mix well to combine.

3 Transfer the bulgur wheat and broccoli mixture to an ovenproof dish and spread out to an even layer. Sprinkle the Gouda on top. Bake for 15–20 minutes or until bubbly at the edges. Remove from the heat and leave to cool slightly. Serve warm.

THAi GREEN CHiCKEN AND MiLLET CURRY
WiTH WiNTER SQUASH

An easy and quick one-pot meal, in this recipe a creamy Thai curry of tender chicken and sweet baked butternut squash is enhanced by the addition of fluffy millet and is perfect for a wholesome lunch or dinner.

SERVES 4 · PREP 15–20 MiNS · COOK 40 MiNS

1 tbsp coconut oil or olive oil

¼ cup Thai green curry paste

2in (5cm) piece of fresh ginger

14oz (400g) boneless chicken thighs, diced

14oz (400ml) can coconut milk

2½ cups chicken stock

1 small butternut squash, seeded and cut into bite-sized pieces

1 cup uncooked millet

salt and freshly ground black pepper

handful of cilantro leaves, to garnish

1 Heat the oil in a large, lidded saucepan over medium-high heat. Add the curry paste and ginger and cook for about 1 minute, stirring frequently. Then add the chicken and cook for another 5 minutes, stirring frequently, until lightly browned.

2 Add the coconut milk, stock, squash, and millet to the pan. Stir to mix and reduce the heat to a simmer. Cover and cook for another 30 minutes or until the chicken is cooked through and the millet and squash are tender. Taste and adjust the seasoning if needed. Remove from the heat. Garnish with cilantro and serve hot.

GRAiN EXCHANGE

This dish also works well with **quinoa**. Use the same quantity of grain as the millet and cook in the same way.

why not try...

You could try adding a small **kabocha squash** in place of the butternut squash, or garnish with **arugula** instead of the cilantro.

SPICY GARLIC QUINOA WITH SEAFOOD STEW

This seafood stew is deceptively simple to make and very satisfying. You can play around with different seafood combinations, trying out varieties that are local, seasonal, and sustainable.

SERVES 4 · PREP 15 MINS, PLUS COOLING · COOK 55 MINS

1 cup uncooked quinoa

pinch of salt

5 tbsp extra virgin olive oil

1 onion, thinly sliced

1 fennel bulb, thinly sliced and fronds reserved

1 large potato, diced into ½ in (1cm) cubes

6 garlic cloves, thinly sliced

6oz (175g) chorizo, diced

4fl oz (120ml) dry white wine

1 tbsp tomato paste

pinch of saffron

14oz (400g) can chopped tomatoes

3 cups chicken stock

¼ tsp chile flakes

1 tsp lemon juice, plus extra to serve

1 tsp grated zest of lemon

12oz (350g) firm white fish, such as halibut, diced

8oz (225g) uncooked shrimp, peeled and deveined

8oz (225g) clams

8oz (225g) mussels

handful of flat-leaf parsley

1 Rinse the quinoa under running water and place in a large saucepan. Cover with 2 cups of water, season with a pinch of salt, and bring to a boil. Reduce the heat to a simmer and cook for about 15 minutes, until tender. Then remove from the heat, drain any remaining water, and leave to cool slightly.

2 For the stew, heat 3 tablespoons of the oil in a large, heavy-bottomed saucepan over medium heat. Add the onions, fennel, and potatoes. Cook for about 10 minutes, stirring frequently, until the onions and fennel have softened and are starting to brown. Then add half the garlic and cook for another 2 minutes.

3 Add the chorizo and cook for 3 minutes, stirring frequently, until browned. Then add the wine and cook until reduced. Add the tomato paste and saffron and stir to combine. Add the tomatoes and stock and bring to a boil. Then reduce the heat to a simmer and cook for about 20 minutes or until the liquid has reduced and the potatoes are soft.

4 Meanwhile, heat the remaining oil in a large frying pan over medium-low heat. Add the chile flakes and the remaining garlic. Cook for about 2 minutes, stirring frequently, until the garlic is fragrant. Add the cooled quinoa and stir to coat with the oil. Remove from the heat, drizzle the lemon juice over it, and toss to combine. Set aside and keep warm.

5 Once the potato is cooked through, add the lemon zest and fish to the stew and cook for another 2–3 minutes. Then add the shrimp, clams, and mussels. Cover and cook until the shrimp are cooked and the mussels and clams are open. Remove from the heat. Take out and discard any mussels and clams that did not open. Place the quinoa in a large serving bowl, top with the seafood stew, and drizzle over some lemon juice. Coarsely chop the parsley and sprinkle it over the stew. Serve immediately.

THAi YELLOW PUMPKiN CURRY WiTH MiLLET

Perfect for vegans, this vibrant curry with its fresh, Thai flavors uses pumpkin and millet to create a hearty and warming dinner that is really comforting in the fall or winter.

SERVES 4–6 · PREP 10 MiNS · COOK 40 MiNS

1 tbsp coconut oil
or canola oil

3 tbsp Thai yellow curry paste

1 onion, finely chopped

1 pumpkin, about 1¾lb (800g),
seeded and chopped into
bite-sized pieces

14oz (400ml) can coconut milk

1¼ cups vegetable stock

1 cup uncooked millet

14oz (400g) can chickpeas,
drained

salt and freshly ground
black pepper

¼ cup chopped cilantro,
to garnish

2 limes, cut into wedges

1 Heat the oil in a large, lidded saucepan over medium heat. Add the curry paste and onions and cook for 2 minutes, stirring frequently. Then add the pumpkin, coconut milk, stock, and millet to the pan. Bring to a simmer, cover, and cook for about 30 minutes.

2 Add the chickpeas and cook for 5 minutes or until the pumpkin is tender. Taste and adjust the seasoning as necessary. Remove from the heat. Garnish with cilantro and serve immediately with lime wedges.

GRAIN EXCHANGE

For a variation, you could use the same amount of **quinoa** in place of the millet.

why not try...

You could try using **butternut squash** in place of the pumpkin, and garnish with **flat-leaf parsley** instead of the cilantro.

SPICY CHICKEN AND SORGHUM STEW

This delicious, warming stew makes excellent use of leftover roasted chicken and is spiced with the inclusion of chorizo. The depth of flavors will vary, based on the use of chorizo made from fresh or smoked pork.

SERVES 4 · PREP 15 MINS · COOK 1 HR 40 MINS

½ cup uncooked sorghum

salt and freshly ground
   black pepper

3 tbsp vegetable oil

6oz (175g) chorizo, diced

1 onion, diced

3 hot red peppers, seeded
   and diced

2 celery ribs, diced

2 carrots, diced

3 garlic cloves, crushed
   and coarsely chopped

1 tbsp tomato paste

3 tbsp all-purpose flour

1 quart chicken stock

1 bay leaf

1lb (450g) roasted chicken,
   shredded

2 scallions, thinly sliced

1 tbsp coarsely chopped
   flat-leaf parsley

1 Place the sorghum in a lidded saucepan and cover with 3 cups of water. Add a pinch of salt, stir to mix, and bring to a boil. Then reduce the heat to a simmer, cover, and cook for 45 minutes or until almost all of the water has been absorbed. Remove from the heat and leave, covered, for about 10 minutes. Then drain any remaining water and set aside.

2 Meanwhile, heat the oil in a large soup pot over medium heat. Add the chorizo and cook, stirring frequently, for 2–3 minutes or until lightly browned. Then add the onions, red peppers, celery, and carrots. Cook for 8–10 minutes, stirring frequently, until the vegetables have softened.

3 Add in the garlic and tomato paste and cook, stirring frequently, for 2 minutes. Then season with ½ teaspoon of salt and a good grinding of pepper. Add the flour, stir well, and cook for 2–3 minutes, stirring constantly.

4 Pour in the stock and add the bay leaf. Bring to a boil, then reduce the heat to a simmer, and cook for another 10 minutes. Then remove the bay leaf. Add the chicken and sorghum and stir to mix. Cook the stew for 20–30 minutes, until thickened. Remove from the heat. Garnish with scallions and parsley and serve hot.

SUMMER BEAN STEW WITH WHEAT BERRIES

Great as a filling lunch or light dinner, this stew is packed with hearty beans and sweet wheat berries. Delicious eaten on its own, this dish can also be served with grilled meats, such as lamb chops.

SERVES 4 · PREP 15 MINS, PLUS OVERNIGHT SOAKING · COOK 55 MINS

½ cup uncooked wheat berries

1 tbsp olive oil

1 onion, finely chopped

2 garlic cloves, finely chopped

2 celery ribs, finely chopped

2 yellow or red bell peppers, seeded and diced

1 zucchini, diced

2 cups vegetable stock

14oz (400g) can navy beans, drained

14oz (400g) can borlotti beans, drained

14oz (400g) can chopped tomatoes

2 tsp Italian herb seasoning

salt and freshly ground black pepper

handful of basil leaves, to garnish

1 Place the wheat berries in a large bowl and cover with water. Leave to soak overnight or for at least 8 hours. Then drain any remaining water and rinse under running water. Drain well and set aside.

2 Heat the oil in a large soup pot over medium heat. Add the onions and garlic and sauté for about 3 minutes or until the onions are translucent. Add the celery and sauté for another 2 minutes. Then add the peppers and zucchini and cook for 3 minutes, stirring frequently.

3 Add the stock, wheat berries, both types of beans, tomatoes, and Italian seasoning. Stir well and reduce the heat to a simmer. Cover and cook for 45 minutes, until the vegetables and wheat berries are tender. Season to taste, if needed, and remove from the heat. Serve hot, garnished with basil.

GRAIN EXCHANGE

This dish works well with a variety of similar grains. Use the same amount of any of the following grains and cook them in the same way as the wheat berries.

kamut

spelt

farro

why not try...

Try using 4–6 **green beans** instead of the zucchini or peppers, and a small handful of **pea shoots**, to garnish, instead of the basil.

COWBOY QUINOA CHILI

This is a modern take on a classic, packed with the flavors of Tex-mex cuisine and the nutty texture of quinoa. Easy to prepare, this chili provides a rich and satisfying meal.

SERVES 4–6 · PREP 15 MINS · COOK 1 HR 10 MINS

1 tbsp olive oil

1 onion, finely chopped

1lb 2oz (500g) lean ground beef

¼ cup taco seasoning

1 cup uncooked quinoa, rinsed

1 red or orange bell pepper, seeded and cut into bite-sized pieces

14oz (400g) can chopped tomatoes

2 cups beef stock

1 tbsp tomato paste

14oz (400g) can black beans, drained

salt and ground black pepper

handful of cilantro, coarsely chopped, to garnish

4–6 tbsp sour cream, to serve

1 Preheat the oven to 350°F (180°C). Heat the oil in a large ovenproof casserole over medium heat. Add the onions and sauté for about 5 minutes, until translucent. Then add the beef and cook for about 5 minutes, stirring frequently, until browned. Add the taco seasoning, stir to mix, and cook for about 2 minutes.

2 Add the quinoa to the casserole and mix to combine. Then add the bell peppers, tomatoes, stock, and tomato paste. Mix well, cover, and place in the oven. Bake for about 30 minutes. Then remove from the oven, stir well to ensure the chili is not sticking to the bottom, and return to the oven for another 15 minutes.

3 Remove the casserole from the oven and add the beans. Mix to combine and return to the oven for another 15 minutes or until the bell peppers are tender and the quinoa is cooked. Remove from the heat and season to taste. Garnish with cilantro and serve hot topped with sour cream.

GRAIN EXCHANGE

For a variation, replace the quinoa with the same amount of **millet**.

why not try...

You could try replacing the black beans with the same quantity of **red kidney beans**.

RED LENTIL AND BULGUR WHEAT KORMA

In this vegan curry, korma paste is used for a light spiciness, along with coconut milk and bulgur wheat for a creamy texture.

SERVES 4 · PREP 5 MINS · COOK 40 MINS

1 tbsp coconut oil	2 cups) vegetable stock
1 onion, finely chopped	7oz (200g) cauliflower, cut into florets
¼ cup korma paste	
¾ cup bulgur wheat	handful of cilantro leaves, to garnish
⅓ cup red lentils	
14oz (400ml) can coconut milk	

1 Heat the oil in a large saucepan over medium heat. Add the onions and cook for 5 minutes, stirring frequently, until translucent. Then add the korma paste and cook, stirring constantly, for about 1 minute. Add the bulgur wheat, lentils, coconut milk, stock, and cauliflower. Mix well to combine.

2 Reduce the heat to a simmer and cook for about 30 minutes, stirring frequently, until the bulgur wheat is cooked, the cauliflower is tender, and the texture is thick and creamy. Remove from the heat, garnish with cilantro, and serve hot.

CAJUN SHRIMP AND SAUSAGE BAKE WITH FREEKEH

A twist on the traditional jambalaya, this dish uses freekeh in place of rice for a spicy yet wholesome and filling dinner.

SERVES 4 · PREP 5 MINS · COOK 50 MINS

8oz (225g) shrimp, peeled and deveined	½ tbsp Cajun seasoning
1 andouille sausage, about 4oz (115g) in total, cut into ¼in (5mm) thin slices	14oz (400g) can chopped tomatoes, with juices
	¾ cup uncooked freekeh
8oz (225g) red potatoes, cut into 1in (2.5cm) pieces	salt and freshly ground black pepper

1 Preheat the oven to 400°F (200°C). Place the shrimp, sausages, and potatoes in an 8 x 11in (20 x 28cm) baking dish. Spread them out in a single layer, sprinkle in the Cajun seasoning, and mix well. Top with the tomatoes and juices and bake in the oven for 40–50 minutes, stirring twice, until the potatoes are tender and cooked through.

2 Meanwhile, place the freekeh in a large, lidded saucepan and cover with 2½ cups of water. Bring to a boil, then reduce the heat to medium-low. Cover and cook for 20–25 minutes. Remove from the heat and drain any remaining water.

3 Transfer the freekeh to a large serving dish, add the shrimp and sausage mixture, and stir well to combine. Season to taste with salt and pepper, if needed, and serve immediately.

BEEF CHIPOTLE CHILI

Inspired by the original Texan chili, this recipe mixes beef with millet for a hearty and filling meal. The chipotle chile turns the sauce into a really spicy mixture, which can be countered with a dollop of cold sour cream.

SERVES 4 · PREP 30 MINS · COOK 1 HR 10 MINS

1–2 tbsp olive oil

1lb (450g) lean ground beef

1lb (450g) ground chuck pieces

1 yellow onion

3 garlic cloves

1 chipotle chile in adobo, plus 1 tsp sauce extra

2 cups tomato sauce

14oz (400g) can chopped tomatoes, with juices

6oz (170g) can tomato paste

1 tbsp chili powder

2 tsp cumin

¼ cup uncooked millet

salt and freshly ground black pepper

handful of cilantro leaves, to garnish (optional)

1 Heat the oil in a Dutch oven or a large casserole over medium heat. Add the ground beef and beef pieces and cook for about 5 minutes, stirring occasionally, until well browned. Drain any excess fat from the pan. Place the onion, garlic, and chipotle chile and sauce in a food processor and pulse until the mixture is almost smooth. Add the mixture to the pot and stir to combine. Cook the mixture for another 5 minutes, stirring frequently.

2 Add the tomato sauce, tomatoes and juices, tomato paste, chili powder, and cumin. Add about ¼ cup of water and stir well to mix. Then reduce the heat to a low simmer, cover, and cook for about 45 minutes. Check the chili occasionally to make sure it does not stick to the pot and add more water if needed.

3 Meanwhile, rinse the millet under cold running water, drain, and place in a small saucepan. Cover with ¾ cup of water and bring to a boil. Then reduce the heat to medium-low, cover, and cook for about 15 minutes. Remove from the heat.

4 Add the millet, along with any remaining water, to the pot and stir well to ensure that it is evenly incorporated. Then cover and cook for another 15–20 minutes. Remove from the heat, taste, and adjust the seasoning if needed. Serve hot, garnished with cilantro, if using.

VEGETABLE DALiA STEW WiTH BULGUR WHEAT

A "dalia" is a soft mix of vegetables and whole grains that is great for the digestion.

SERVES 6 · PREP 10 MiNS · COOK 1 HR

1 tbsp olive oil	1½ cups bulgur wheat
1 onion, finely chopped	½ cup red lentils
1½ tsp ground turmeric	1½ quarts vegetable stock
2 celery ribs, chopped into small pieces	salt and freshly ground black pepper
1 carrot, cut into small pieces	6 tbsp coarsely chopped cilantro leaves, to garnish
7oz (200g) potato, cut into ¾in (2cm) cubes	
5½oz (150g) cauliflower, cut into florets	

1 Heat the oil in a large soup pot over medium heat. Add the onions and sauté for 5 minutes. Add the turmeric and cook, stirring frequently, for 1 minute. Then stir in the celery, carrots, potatoes, and cauliflower. Mix well and cook for 1 minute.

2 Add the bulgur wheat, lentils, and stock to the pot and mix well to combine. Reduce the heat to a simmer, cover, and cook for 50 minutes or until the vegetables are tender and the bulgur wheat is cooked. Season to taste, stir well, and remove from the heat. Garnish with cilantro and serve hot.

SLOW COOKER BEEF AND VEGETABLE STEW

This warming, slow cooker dish is as easy to make as it is satisfying.

SERVES 6 · PREP 20 MiNS · COOK 12 HRS

¼ cup all-purpose flour	3 carrots, diced
salt and freshly ground black pepper	6 garlic cloves, roasted, sliced, and crushed
1¼lb (550g) stew beef, cut into 1in (2.5cm) chunks	½ cup uncooked kamut
1 onion, diced	1 quart beef stock
2 potatoes, diced	9fl oz (250ml) red wine

1 Place the flour in a shallow dish and season with salt and pepper. Add the beef and toss to coat. Place the beef, onions, potatoes, carrots, garlic, and kamut in a slow cooker and mix well.

2 Pour in the stock and wine, season to taste, and stir lightly to mix. Place the cooker on low heat and cook for 10–12 hours. Then remove from the heat and serve hot. Store the leftovers in an airtight container in the fridge for up to five days.

AMARANTH AND WHITE BEAN CHILI

This rich, creamy vegetarian chili gets its heartiness from the amaranth, which works brilliantly as a thickener and combines well with the cannellini beans to give this dish an earthy flavor.

SERVES 4 · PREP 10 MINS · COOK 40 MINS

3 tbsp canola oil

3 onions, diced

2 poblano chiles, seeded and diced

6 garlic cloves, crushed

2 x 14oz (400g) can cannellini beans

1¼ cups chopped cilantro leaves, plus extra to garnish

1 tbsp oregano

¼ tsp cayenne pepper

½ tsp ground cumin

salt and freshly ground black pepper

3 cups vegetable stock

1 cup whole milk

¼ cup uncooked amaranth

2⅓ cups sour cream or plain Greek yogurt, plus extra to serve

1 Heat the oil in a large, heavy-bottomed saucepan over medium heat. Add the onions and poblano chiles and cook for about 5 minutes, stirring occasionally, until the onions are translucent. Then add the garlic and cook for another 2 minutes.

2 Add the cannellini beans, cilantro, oregano, cayenne pepper, and cumin to the pan. Season with ¼ teaspoon of salt, stir to mix, and cook for about 1 minute. Then add the stock, milk, and amaranth. Mix well and bring to a boil.

3 Reduce the heat to a simmer and cook for about 30 minutes or until it reduces and thickens. Add the sour cream and stir to combine. Remove from the heat and taste and adjust the seasoning, if needed. Serve warm, garnished with cilantro.

onions

RED WINE-BRAISED BEETS AND LENTILS WITH FARRO

Beet and lentils are a match made in heaven when braised in a full-bodied red wine. Be sure to use a wine of good quality, as it will enhance the flavor of the stew and you can save a glass to have with your meal.

SERVES 4 · PREP 30 MINS, PLUS OVERNIGHT SOAKING AND CHILLING · COOK 1 HR 20 MINS

¾ cup uncooked farro

3 tbsp olive oil

1 garlic clove, sliced

salt and freshly ground black pepper

1 cup Greek yogurt

1 tbsp lemon juice

1 tsp lemon zest

1 small garlic clove, crushed

1 tbsp extra virgin olive oil

handful of flat-leaf parsley

FOR THE LENTILS AND VEGETABLES

1 onion, finely sliced

3 garlic cloves, crushed

3 large beets, peeled and chopped into 1in (3cm) pieces

2 carrots, chopped into 1in (2.5cm) pieces

2 tsp tomato paste

3½oz (100g) black beluga lentils, rinsed and cleaned

7fl oz (200ml) good-quality red wine, such as a cabernet

1 cup vegetable stock

sprig each of rosemary and thyme

1 bay leaf

1 Place the farro in a large bowl, cover with water, and leave to soak overnight or for up to 12 hours. Then drain and rinse under running water. Drain well.

2 Heat 1 tablespoon of the light olive oil in a saucepan over medium heat. Add the farro and sliced garlic. Season to taste with salt and cook for 5 minutes, stirring occasionally, until the farro is lightly toasted. Add 1 quart of water and bring to a boil. Then reduce the heat to a simmer, cover, and cook for 25–30 minutes or until the farro is tender. Drain any remaining water and rinse under running water. Drain well and set aside.

3 For the lentils and vegetables, heat the remaining light olive oil in a large, heavy-bottomed, lidded saucepan over medium heat. Add the onions and cook for 2–3 minutes or until softened. Then add the garlic, beets, and carrots. Season to taste with a good grinding of pepper and cook for 5–10 minutes, stirring occasionally. Add the tomato paste in a corner of the pan, cook for 1–2 minutes, then stir to mix with the vegetables.

4 Add the lentils, wine, stock, rosemary, thyme, and bay leaf. Bring to a boil. Then reduce the heat to a simmer and cook, covered, for 25 minutes or until the lentils and vegetables are cooked through. Season with salt and cook for another 5–10 minutes. Remove from the heat and discard the rosemary, thyme, and bay leaf.

5 Place the yogurt, lemon juice, lemon zest, crushed garlic, and extra virgin olive oil in a bowl. Finely chop the parsley and add to the bowl. Season with a pinch of salt and whisk to combine. Cover with plastic wrap and chill for 15 minutes. To serve, divide the farro between four serving plates, top with the beets and lentils, and spoon a dollop of yogurt on top.

ALL THINGS SWEET

PUFFED SORGHUM SALTED CARAMEL POPCORN BALLS

This easy-to-make recipe uses sugar-free caramel, pecans, and popped sorghum to transform a popular snack into a delightful sweet and salty homemade treat that everyone will enjoy.

MAKES 12 BALLS · PREP 15 MINS, PLUS COOLING · COOK 20 MINS

½ cup uncooked sorghum

1 tbsp vegetable oil

2½oz (75g) corn kernels

1 cup pecans,
   coarsely chopped

FOR THE CARAMEL

½ cup maple syrup

2 tbsp unsalted butter

1 tsp apple cider vinegar

½ tsp salt

1 Heat a large, lidded saucepan over medium heat for 5–10 minutes. Add half the sorghum to the pan and cover. Shake the pan lightly at regular intervals until the grain starts to pop. Remove the sorghum when the popping stops or slows to less than every 5 seconds. Repeat with the remaining sorghum. Place the popped grain in a large bowl and set aside to cool.

2 Increase the heat to medium-high and pour the oil into the pan. Once the oil is hot, add one-third of the corn kernels, cover, and shake the pan lightly to help them pop. Remove the popped corn and repeat with the remaining kernels. Remove from the heat and add to the popped sorghum. Leave to cool for 5 minutes. Then sift through to remove any hard kernels or sorghum grains. Add the pecans and mix well to combine.

3 For the caramel, heat a nonstick frying pan over medium-high heat. Add the maple syrup, butter, apple cider vinegar, and ¼ cup of water. Bring to a boil, then reduce to a simmer. Cook for 10 minutes, stirring occasionally, until reduced to a thick and sticky caramel. Make sure the ingredients do not splash out of the pan as they will be hot.

4 Remove from the heat and leave to cool for about 2 minutes. Then add the salt and stir to mix. Pour over the sorghum, popcorn, and pecan mixture. Mix to coat and leave to cool. When cool enough to handle, form the mixture into 12 balls, pressing firmly to ensure that they stick. Place the balls on a baking sheet to cool and harden. Store in an airtight container.

STRAWBERRY POLENTA SHORTCAKES

These little "sandwiches" are a lovely adaptation of the traditional shortcake. They make excellent use of polenta to produce the perfect dessert for summer, when you can take advantage of a glut of strawberries.

SERVES 6 · PREP 30 MINS · COOK 40 MINS

1¼ cups polenta

2 tbsp olive oil

3 tbsp sugar

1 tsp vanilla extract

1¼ cups heavy cream

1lb 2oz (500g) strawberries

3 tbsp confectioners' sugar

1 Preheat the oven to 375°F (190°C). Line two baking sheets with parchment paper and set aside. Place 1 quart of water in a large saucepan and bring to a simmer. Then add the polenta and cook for 2–3 minutes, stirring constantly, until it has thickened. Remove from the heat and leave to cool for about 2 minutes.

2 Add the oil, sugar, and vanilla extract and mix well. Divide the mixture equally between the two baking sheets, spreading it out to a ¼in (5mm) thick layer. Place the sheets in the oven and bake for 30 minutes or until the polenta is spongy and slightly firm to the touch. It should easily pull away from the paper. Remove from the heat and leave to cool.

3 Place the cooled polenta on a clean work surface and use a cookie cutter to cut out twelve 3in (8cm) wide rounds. Place the heavy cream in a large bowl and whisk until it is thick and holds its shape. Place one-third of the strawberries in a bowl and crush with the back of a fork. Add half the confectioners' sugar and mix well to combine. Cut the remaining strawberries into thin slices.

4 To assemble the shortcakes, lay one polenta round on each of six plates. Top them with 1 tablespoon of the whipped cream, 1 tablespoon of the strawberry and sugar mixture, and a few slices of strawberries. Place the remaining polenta rounds on top and gently pat them dry with paper towels. Dust with confectioners' sugar and serve immediately.

GOAT CHEESECAKE WiTH AN ALMOND AND AMARANTH CRUST

This decadent dessert is given a healthy twist with the addition of yogurt and a wholesome crust made from earthy amaranth and crunchy almonds. Easy to make, the hardest part is waiting for the cake to set before serving yourself a slice.

SERVES 8–12 · PREP 10 MiNS, PLUS COOLiNG · COOK 55 MiNS

1lb 5oz (600g) goat cheese, softened

8oz (225g) cream cheese, softened

¾ cup sugar

1 cup plain, low-fat Greek yogurt

1½ tsp vanilla extract

4 eggs

FOR THE BASE

1 cup ground almonds

⅓ cup amaranth flour

½ cup tapioca starch

½ cup confectioners' sugar

½ tsp salt

½ cup butter, melted

1 Preheat the oven to 350°F (180°C). Grease a 9in (23cm) springform cake pan. For the base, place all the ingredients in a bowl and mix to combine. Press the mixture into the bottom of the pan, making sure it is evenly covered. Set aside.

2 Place the goat cheese, cream cheese, and sugar in a food processor and pulse to combine. Then add the yogurt and vanilla extract and pulse until just incorporated. Scrape down the sides of the bowl and stir well. Add the eggs, one at a time, and pulse until thoroughly blended. Pour the mixture over the base and transfer the pan to the oven.

3 Bake the cake for 25 minutes. Then rotate it by 180 degrees and bake for another 20–30 minutes, until the top is wobbly but set. If it starts to brown too quickly, cover loosely with a sheet of foil. Remove from the heat. Leave the cake in the pan to cool down to room temperature. Gently remove from the pan and serve.

BAKED APPLES STUFFED WITH KAMUT AND RAISINS

Like the traditional baked apples, this recipe is both delicious and healthy, with the added bonus of whole grain kamut that brings with it a chewy texture and a nutty flavor.

SERVES 4 · PREP 15 MINS, PLUS SOAKING AND COOLING · COOK 1 HR 30 MINS

⅓ cup uncooked kamut

6 apples, such as Granny Smith

½ cup raisins

2 tsp ground cinnamon

¼ cup honey

½ cup unsalted butter

1 Place the kamut in a bowl, cover with water, and leave to soak for about 8 hours or for up to 24 hours. Then drain, rinse under running water, and drain well again.

2 Place the kamut in a saucepan and cover with water. Bring to a boil, then reduce the heat to a simmer, and cook for 40–45 minutes. Remove from the heat, drain any remaining water, and leave to cool.

3 Preheat the oven to 320°F (160°C). Remove the cores from the apples, keeping the bottom ½in (1cm) intact. Make the hole in the center of each apple about 1in (2.5cm) wide. Place the apples in a large, deep-sided, ovenproof casserole.

4 Place the raisins, cinnamon, honey, and half of the butter in a bowl and mix to combine. Then add the cooled kamut and mix until evenly combined. Stuff the apples with equal quantities of the mixture. Top with the remaining butter.

5 Bake in the oven for 45 minutes—1 hour, until tender and easily pierced with a knife. Check every 15 minutes and spoon any melting butter on top of the kamut to keep it soft and to prevent it from becoming crisp. Remove from the heat and serve warm.

GRAIN EXCHANGE
For a variation, use the same amount of any of the following grains in place of the kamut.

wheat berries

spelt

farro

why not try...
Try using the same amount of chopped **dates** in place of the raisins. You could also try adding ¼ cup of finely chopped **walnuts**.

ROASTED FRUIT WITH MILLET CRUMBLE

The traditional crumble dessert gets a makeover, because roasting fruit brings out its natural sweetness with no need for added sugar, while the millet and almonds create a crisp, gluten-free crumble topping.

SERVES 4–6 · PREP 15 MINS, PLUS COOLING · COOK 1 HR

FOR THE FILLING

1¾lb (800g) mixed fruit, such as peaches, nectarines, and plums, pitted and coarsely chopped

1 tbsp coconut oil, room temperature

FOR THE CRUMBLE TOPPING

2 cups millet flakes

¾ cup ground almonds

¼ cup coconut oil, chilled and diced

⅓ cup unrefined sugar

1 Preheat the oven to 400°F (200°C). For the filling, place the fruit in a roasting tray, drizzle the oil over it, and toss to coat. Roast in the oven for 20–30 minutes, until tender but still holding their shape. Remove from the oven and leave to cool for at least 10 minutes.

2 For the crumble topping, place the millet flakes and almonds in a bowl and mix well to combine. Rub in the oil and mix well until the mixture resembles rough bread crumbs. Add the sugar and gently mix to combine.

3 Place the cooled fruit mixture in an 8 x 10in (20 x 25cm) shallow baking dish and spread it out in an even layer. Sprinkle the topping evenly over the fruit. Place in the oven and bake for 20–30 minutes, until the topping is golden brown. Remove from the heat and serve warm.

GRAIN EXCHANGE

You could also use the same amount of **quinoa flakes** instead of the millet flakes.

why not try...

For an alternative, try using the same amount of **apples** and **blackberries** in place of the suggested fruit.

CREAMY COCONUT BARLEY
WiTH STRAWBERRY CHiA JAM

Forget the typical rice pudding, as this new, healthier version combines delicious coconut milk with the grainy goodness of barley, along with super-food chia seeds, making it a great vegan dessert.

SERVES 4 · PREP 10 MiNS, PLUS OVERNiGHT SOAKiNG AND CHiLLiNG · COOK 30 MiNS

1¼ cups uncooked pearl barley

2½ cups coconut milk, plus extra if needed

⅓ cup honey

FOR THE JAM

14oz (400g) strawberries, stalks removed

2 tbsp honey

¼ cup chia seeds

1 Place the pearl barley in a bowl, cover with water, and leave to soak overnight or for up to 8 hours. Then drain, rinse under running water, and drain well again.

2 For the jam, place the strawberries in a large bowl and roughly mash with the back of a fork so that they release some juices but still retain some texture. Add the honey and chia seeds and mix well to combine. Chill in the fridge until thickened.

3 Place the barley, coconut milk, and honey in a large, lidded saucepan and bring to a boil. Then reduce the heat to a simmer, cover, and cook for 25–30 minutes or until the barley is tender, but still chewy, and the mixture has reached a thick oatmeal-like consistency. Check frequently and add more milk if the mixture seems too dry or if the liquid is absorbed too quickly. Remove from the heat. Divide the barley between four dishes. Top with 2–3 tablespoons of the jam and serve warm or at room temperature.

strawberries

CHOCOLATE AND AMARANTH PUDDING

Minty chocolate pudding and whipped cream make a decadent dessert that your family will love.

SERVES 4 · PREP 10 MINS · COOK 30 MINS

⅓ cup uncooked amaranth	½ tsp mint extract
⅓ cup granulated sugar	½ cup heavy cream
⅓ cup unsweetened cocoa powder	2 tbsp confectioners' sugar
2 tbsp cornstarch	½ tsp vanilla extract
1½ cups milk	

1 Place 1 cup of water in a lidded saucepan and bring to a boil. Add the amaranth, cover, and reduce the heat to medium-low. Cook for about 20 minutes or until all the water has been absorbed. Remove from the heat and set side.

2 Meanwhile, in a separate saucepan, place the sugar, cocoa powder, cornstarch, and milk. Mix to combine and bring to a boil over medium heat, stirring constantly. Then reduce the heat to low and cook for 2 minutes, until thickened. Remove from the heat, add the mint extract, and stir to combine.

3 Divide the pudding into two equal parts. Stir the amaranth into one half of the pudding, allow to cool slightly, and divide evenly between four tall glasses. Top each with the remaining half of the pudding.

4 Place the heavy cream, confectioners' sugar, and vanilla extra in a bowl and use a handheld blender to process until light and fluffy. Top each pudding with one-quarter of the cream and serve immediately.

SPICED FRUITY MILLET CAKE

Just right for family and friends, this delicious cake will disappear in an instant.

SERVES 8-9 · PREP 10 MINS · COOK 50 MINUTES

¾ cup couscous	1 large egg, beaten
½ cup uncooked millet	2 tsp ground cinnamon
⅔ cup raisins	1 tsp grated fresh ginger
1½ cups strawberry yogurt	

1 Place the couscous in a bowl and cover with ⅔ cup of boiling water. Cover with a plate and leave to sit.

2 Rinse the millet and place in a saucepan with 1 cup of water. Bring to a boil, then reduce the heat to a simmer. Cook for 15–20 minutes or until all the water has been absorbed and the millet is tender and fluffy. Remove from the heat and leave to cool.

3 Preheat the oven to 400°F (200°C). Grease and line a 9in (23cm) square baking dish with parchment paper. Add the couscous to the millet and fluff together with a fork, breaking up any lumps that have formed.

4 Add the raisins, yogurt, egg, and spices to the millet and couscous. Mix well to combine and transfer to the prepared dish. Smooth over the top and bake in the oven for 30 minutes, until it is firm to the touch and golden, and a skewer inserted into the center comes out clean. Remove from the heat and serve warm.

SWEET SPICED FREEKEH
WITH FRESH FIGS

Inspired by the cuisine of the Middle East, in this dish the freekeh is cooked with sweet spices to enhance its flavor and served with honey, pistachios, and figs for an aromatic and mouth-watering dessert.

SERVES 4 · PREP 5 MINS · COOK 25 MINS

½ cup cracked freekeh

1 star anise

4 cardamom pods

1 tsp ground cinnamon

½ tsp grated fresh ginger

¼ tsp grated nutmeg

¼ tsp salt

8 fresh figs, stems removed

¼ cup honey, plus extra to serve

⅓ cup pistachios, coarsely chopped

2 tbsp chopped mint leaves

¼ cup Greek yogurt, to serve

1 Place the freekeh, star anise, cardamom, cinnamon, ginger, and nutmeg in a large saucepan. Add the salt and cover with 2 cups of water. Place the pan over medium heat and bring to a boil. Then reduce the heat to a simmer and cook for about 15 minutes or until all the liquid has been absorbed.

2 Meanwhile, preheat the broiler to its medium setting. Grease and line a baking sheet with parchment paper. Cut a cross in the top of each fig, cutting almost to the bottom so they open up like a flower. Place on the baking sheet and drizzle with 2 tablespoons of honey. Place the sheet under the broiler and cook for 10 minutes or until the figs are lightly broiled.

3 Remove and discard the star anise and cardamom pods. Add the remaining honey to the cooked freekeh and mix well. Divide the freekeh mixture between four plates. Top each plate with two figs and a quarter of the pistachios. Garnish with mint and drizzle with honey, if you wish. Serve with Greek yogurt.

GRAIN EXCHANGE

In place of the freekeh, use the same quantity of either of the following grains.

teff

polenta

CHOCOLATE, HAZELNUT, AND BUCKWHEAT CAKE

Buckwheat flour naturally complements the creamy chocolate and subtle hazelnut and vanilla flavoring in this decadent cake. Serve it as it is, or with a scoop of vanilla ice cream for the perfect after-dinner indulgence.

MAKES 1 · PREP 30 MiNS · COOK 35 MiNS

7 tbsp butter, melted, plus extra for greasing

½ cup hazelnuts

3½oz (100g) dark chocolate, at least 70 percent cocoa solids, broken into pieces

4 large eggs, lightly beaten

½ cup coconut palm sugar or brown sugar

¼ tsp sea salt

1 tsp vanilla extract

¼ cup buckwheat flour

1 Preheat the oven to 350°F (180°C). Grease and line a 9in (23cm) cake pan with parchment paper. Place the hazelnuts on a baking sheet and roast in the oven for about 5 minutes or until they are lightly browned and the skins have loosened. Remove from the heat and leave to cool.

2 Once cool enough to handle, lightly rub the hazelnuts between your hands, or a dish towel, to remove the skins. Place them in a food processor and pulse until reduced to a coarse flour. Remove from the food processor and set aside.

3 Place the chocolate in a bowl and set over a pan of simmering water to melt. Place the eggs, sugar, and salt in a bowl and whisk until the mixture doubles in size. Then gently fold in the vanilla extract, butter, and melted chocolate. Add the hazelnut flour and buckwheat flour and gently fold the batter to incorporate all the ingredients.

4 Spoon the batter into the cake pan, in a smooth and even layer. Bake for about 30 minutes or until a skewer inserted into the center comes out clean. Remove from the heat and leave to cool in the pan. Then transfer the cake to a serving platter and serve at room temperature.

LAVENDER AND LEMON BARS WITH A SPELT CRUST

A slight twist on the classic lemon bars, this recipe uses lavender, tapioca, and spelt flour in the crust to add a floral and earthy note to this heavenly dessert.

MAKES 18 · PREP 15 MINS, PLUS CHILLING · COOK 40 MINS

FOR THE CRUST

1 cup spelt flour

⅓ cup tapioca starch

½ cup confectioners' sugar

½ tsp salt

1 tbsp finely chopped lavender

1 tsp grated lemon zest

½ cup butter, chilled and diced, plus extra for greasing

FOR THE FILLING

1¼ cups sugar

4 eggs

½ cup lemon juice

⅓ cup spelt flour

¼ tsp salt

1 tsp vanilla extract

2 tbsp confectioners' sugar, for dusting

1 Preheat the oven to 350°F (180°C). Grease an 8 x 11in (20 x 28cm) baking pan. For the crust, place the flour, starch, sugar, salt, lavender, and lemon zest in a large bowl and mix well. Then add the butter and rub it in until the mixture resembles coarse bread crumbs.

2 Transfer the mixture to the baking pan and spread it out in an even layer. Place the pan in the oven and bake for about 20 minutes or until lightly browned. Remove from the heat and set aside. Reduce the oven temperature to 325°F (160°C).

3 Meanwhile, for the filling, place the sugar and eggs in a bowl and cream together using a handheld blender, until it turns a pale yellow. Then add the lemon juice, flour, salt, and vanilla extract to the bowl. Beat the ingredients until well combined.

4 Pour the custard mixture over the crust and bake for another 20 minutes or until the filling has set. Remove from the heat and leave to cool, until it reaches room temperature. Then transfer to an airtight container and chill in the fridge for at least 1 hour. Serve chilled, dusted with confectioners' sugar.

ALMOND POLENTA CAKE
WiTH RASPBERRiES

This gluten-free cake is perfect for satisfying your sweet tooth while staying away from flour. The polenta and almonds give the cake a crumbly texture that beautifully offsets the tartness of the raspberries.

SERVES 8-10 · PREP 15 MiNS, PLUS COOLiNG · COOK 45 MiNS

14 tbsp unsalted butter

1¼ cups unrefined sugar

3 large eggs

1 tsp almond extract

2 cups ground almonds

⅔ cup polenta

1½ tsp baking powder

7oz (200g) raspberries

¼ cup slivered almonds

1 Preheat the oven to 350°F (180°C). Grease and line a 9in (23cm) springform cake pan with parchment paper. Cream the butter and sugar with an electric whisk for 2 minutes or until light and fluffy. Add the eggs one at a time, mixing well between additions. Then add the almond extract and whisk for 2 minutes until fully incorporated.

2 Place the ground almonds, polenta, and baking powder in a separate bowl and mix well. Lightly fold the dry mixture into the butter, sugar, and egg mixture until just smooth. Gently fold the raspberries into the batter. Spoon the batter into the prepared pan, smooth over the surface, and scatter the flaked almonds over it.

3 Bake the cake for 45 minutes or until golden brown and a skewer inserted into the center comes out with only a few crumbs. Leave the cake in the pan to cool slightly. Then transfer to a wire rack to cool completely before serving. Store in the fridge, in an airtight container, for up to 3 days.

LEMON AND BLUEBERRY BULGUR WHEAT BAKE

The lemon and blueberries create a tangy duo in this delightfully light and creamy bake that uses bulgur wheat as its base. it's perfect for a lunch party as an alternative to summer dessert.

SERVES 6–8 · PREP 10 MiNS · COOK 1 HR 15 MiNUTES

1½ cups bulgur wheat

1 tbsp unsalted butter

2 large eggs

½ cup milk

grated zest of 3 lemons

½ cup unrefined sugar

7oz (200g) blueberries

1 Place the bulgur wheat in a large saucepan and cover with 2 cups of water. Bring to a boil, then reduce the heat to a simmer, and cover. Cook for about 15 minutes or until all the water is absorbed and the bulgur wheat is tender. Remove from the heat and set aside to cool.

2 Preheat the oven to 350°F (180°C). Grease a 6 cup (1.5 liter) ovenproof dish with the butter and set aside. Place the eggs and milk in a bowl. Whisk to combine, then add the lemon zest, and whisk again until well incorporated.

3 Place the bulgur wheat in a separate large bowl. Add the sugar and blueberries and mix well. Then add the egg and milk mixture and mix until well incorporated. Transfer the mixture to the prepared dish and bake for 1 hour, until golden on top and just set in the middle. Serve warm, with whipped cream or yogurt.

GRAiN EXCHANGE

You could replace the bulgur wheat with the same amount of **freekeh**.

why not try...

Instead of blueberries, you could use the same amount of **raspberries**.

SPELT AND OLiVE OiL CAKE

This filling cake is flavored by the unique combination of olive oil and blood orange juice. You could also use a different or seasonal citrus fruit such as Meyer lemons for the same result.

SERVES 12 · PREP 10 MiNS, PLUS COOLiNG AND SETTiNG · COOK 40 MiNS

½ cup extra virgin olive oil,
  plus extra for greasing

1½ cup spelt flour

1 cup ground almonds

grated zest of 1 blood orange

2 tsp baking powder

1 tsp salt

½ cup blood orange juice

2 eggs

¾ cup brown sugar

FOR THE GLAZE

1 tsp blood orange juice

⅓ cup confectioners' sugar

1 Preheat the oven to 350°F (180°C). Grease and line a 9in (23cm) round cake pan with parchment paper. Place the spelt flour, ground almonds, blood orange zest, baking powder, and salt in a bowl and mix well until combined.

2 Place the oil, blood orange juice, eggs, and sugar in a separate bowl. Whisk to combine. Make a well in the center of the dry ingredients and pour in the oil mixture. Mix until just incorporated, making sure you don't over-mix the batter.

3 Transfer the mixture to the prepared cake pan. Bake for 35–40 minutes or until the top of the cake is golden brown and a skewer inserted into the center comes out clean. Remove from the heat and leave to rest for about 10 minutes. Then carefully flip the cake out of the pan and transfer to a wire rack to cool slightly.

4 Meanwhile, for the glaze, place the blood orange juice, confectioners' sugar, and 2 teaspoons of water in a bowl and whisk to combine. Pour the glaze over the cake and leave to set. Serve warm.

CHOCOLATE CHIP, PEANUT, AND BUCKWHEAT COOKIES

Gluten-free buckwheat flour adds to the nuttiness of these delicious cookies. Perfect for children and adults alike, enjoy them with a glass of milk or even your afternoon coffee!

MAKES 12 LARGE COOKIES · PREP 30 MINUTES, PLUS CHILLING AND COOLING · COOK 15 MINUTES

½ cup unsalted butter

1 cup brown sugar

1 large egg

1⅓ cups buckwheat flour

¼ tsp salt

½ tsp baking soda

3oz (85g) dark chocolate chips

½ cup salted peanuts

1 Line two baking sheets with parchment paper and set aside. In a large bowl, cream together the butter and sugar with an electric whisk until light and fluffy. Then beat the egg into the mixture until well combined.

2 Place the flour, salt, and baking powder in a separate bowl and mix well. Fold the dry mixture into the butter, sugar, and egg mixture, a little at a time, until thoroughly incorporated. Add the chocolate chips and peanuts to the mixture and stir well to incorporate. Cover the dough with plastic wrap and chill in the fridge for about 30 minutes. Preheat the oven to 350°F (180°C).

3 Place golf ball-sized pieces of the dough on the prepared baking sheets and flatten them gently. Make sure they are placed at least 2in (5cm) apart, as they will spread while baking. Bake the cookies for about 15 minutes, until they start to turn golden but still look a little under baked. Remove from the oven and leave on the baking sheet for at least 10 minutes to cool and firm up. Then transfer to a wire rack to cool completely. Store in an airtight container.

GRiLLED PEACHES WiTH iCE CREAM AND WHOLE GRAiN GRANOLA

Grilled peaches are one of summer's tastiest treats. Paired here with a healthy amaranth and millet granola, they are easy to prepare and can also be stored overnight for a filling whole grain breakfast.

SERVES 4 · PREP 10 MiNS · COOK 20 MiNS

4 peaches, pitted and halved

2 tbsp canola oil

4 scoops of vanilla ice cream

FOR THE GRANOLA

⅔ cup oats

¼ cup uncooked amaranth

¼ cup uncooked millet

¾ cup almonds, chopped

⅓ cup pumpkin seeds

1 tbsp virgin coconut oil

2 tbsp maple syrup

½ tsp vanilla extract

¼ tsp ground cinnamon

¼ tsp sea salt

1 Preheat the oven to 350°F (180°C). For the granola, place all the ingredients in a large bowl and toss to combine. Spread the mixture evenly in a baking tray and place in the oven. Bake the granola for 10–15 minutes or until the oats and nuts are lightly browned. Remove from the heat and leave to cool.

2 Meanwhile, set the broiler at its medium setting. Brush the peach skins with the oil and place under the broiler for 2–3 minutes, on each side, until tender. Remove from the heat. Place the grilled peaches in serving dishes, then top with a scoop of vanilla ice cream, and some of the granola. Serve immediately.

STRAWBERRY AND PEACH GALETTE WITH WHEAT BERRIES

Literally meaning a flat crusty cake, a galette is perfectly accompanied by summer fruit such as strawberries and peaches. The wheat berries in this recipe give the pastry a fresh taste and a hearty, crunchy texture.

SERVES 6 · PREP 25 MINS, PLUS CHILLING AND SOAKING · COOK 40–45 MINS

1 cup soft wheat berries

1 tbsp sugar

¼ tsp salt

½ cup unsalted butter, chilled and diced

FOR THE FILLING

2 ripe peaches, pitted and sliced

10oz (300g) strawberries, trimmed and halved

2 tbsp honey

½ tsp orange juice or lemon juice

1 tsp vanilla extract

1 Place the wheat berries in a coffee grinder and grind into a fine flour. Sift the flour into a bowl, removing any remaining hard pieces. Transfer 1 cup of the flour to a large bowl, reserving the remaining flour for dusting. Add the sugar and salt to the flour and mix well. Rub in the butter and combine until the mixture resembles rough bread crumbs.

2 Add 3–4 tablespoons of chilled water, a little at a time, and combine with the flour mixture until it forms a dough. Form the dough into a ball and lightly press into a disklike shape. Cover the dough with plastic wrap and chill in the fridge for 30 minutes.

3 Meanwhile, for the filling, place all the ingredients in a large bowl and mix well. Leave for about 20 minutes, to draw the water out. Preheat the oven to 350°F (180°C) and line a baking sheet with parchment paper.

4 On a lightly floured surface, roll out the pastry to a 10in (25cm) circle. If the pastry is too hard, allow it to reach room temperature and soften before rolling it out. Drain and discard the liquid from the fruit mixture. Place the fruit in the center of the pastry circle. Then fold up the pastry to enclose the fruit, and crimp the edges with your fingers to decorate.

5 Bake in the oven for 40–45 minutes or until the crust is golden brown and the fruit is bubbling. Remove from the oven and leave to cool slightly. Serve warm.

WHOLE GRAIN CHOCOLATE CHIP PIE

This pie-version of your favorite chocolate chip cookie is also full of wholesome goodness and is best served warm with a big scoop of vanilla ice cream for a delicious treat.

SERVES 6 · PREP 20 MINUTES, PLUS COOLING AND CHILLING · COOK 1 HR 30 MINS

¼ cup uncooked amaranth

2 large eggs

⅔ cup whole wheat flour

½ tsp salt

½ cup granulated sugar

½ cup brown sugar

12 tbsp butter, softened

1 tbsp vanilla extract

10oz (300g) chocolate chips

confectioners' sugar, for dusting

FOR THE CRUST

6oz (175g) graham crackers

⅓ cup demerara sugar

6 tbsp butter, melted

1 Preheat the oven to 350°F (180°C). For the crust, crush the graham crackers by hand or pulse in a food processor until they resemble fine bread crumbs. Place the crumbs in a large bowl and add the sugar and butter. Mix until the mixture resembles wet sand.

2 Spoon the mixture into a 9in (23cm) loose-bottomed tart pan. Press the mixture firmly into the bottom and sides of the pan, making sure it is as packed as possible and there is a good side to the crust. Place the crust on a baking sheet and bake for about 10 minutes. Remove from the oven and set aside to cool before chilling for at least 30 minutes.

3 Meanwhile, place the amaranth in a small saucepan and cover with 1 cup of water. Bring to a simmer and cook for about 40 minutes or until all the water has been absorbed. Drain any remaining water and rinse under running water. Set aside.

4 Place the eggs in a large bowl and process with a handheld blender for about 3 minutes or until foamy. Add the flour, salt, and both sugars. Beat the mixture until just combined. Then add the butter and vanilla extract and beat until well incorporated.

5 Add the amaranth and chocolate chips to the bowl and mix until evenly combined. Spoon the mixture into the crust and spread into one even layer. Bake in the oven for 40 minutes, until a skewer inserted into it comes out clean. Transfer to a wire rack to cool. Dust with confectioners' sugar and serve warm.

iNDEX

Entries in **bold** indicate ingredients.

ACKNOWLEDGMENTS

ABOUT THE AUTHORS

JODI MORENO is a chef and food photographer who runs the food blog *What's Cooking Good Looking*. Her work has been featured on countless sites, such as the *Huffington Post*, *Edible Magazine*, *Food52*, *Gourmet*, *Self Magazine*, *Buzzfeed*, *The Kitchn*, and *VegNews Magazine*. She was named by *Better Homes and Gardens* and *Shape Magazine* as one of the best healthy food bloggers, and *Saveur Magazine* selected her blog as one of the best overall blogs of 2014.

SARAH W. CARON is the senior features editor for the *Bangor Daily News* and a freelance writer, editor, and recipe developer. In addition to her newspaper column, Maine Course, she's written for publications including *Bella*, *Connecticut Magazine*, *Betty Crocker*, and *iVillage*. She also writes the food blog *sarahscucinabella.com*, which was voted one of the Top 25 foodie blogs by *FriendsEat* in 2009 and named as one of the "Sites We Love" by *Saveur Magazine*.

LAURA AGAR WILSON is a health coach, writer, recipe developer, and author of the popular healthy living and lifestyle blog *wholeheartedlyhealthy.com*, where she shares healthy living tips and tricks, recipes, and her own personal healthy living journey. Her work has featured on *BBC Good Food*, *Grazia Daily*, and *Channel 4 Food* websites. She also writes regularly for the *Huffington Post* and has appeared in *Healthy Magazine* as a Healthy Hero.

THANKS

Jodi Moreno would like to thank her husband, Michael Moreno, for his endless support and washing of dishes.

Laura Agar Wilson would like to thank the team at DK "for involving me in this project and supporting me throughout"; her husband, James, for putting up with a very hectic and messy kitchen, and her best friend, Claire, for her support and feedback on recipes.

DK would like to thank the following:
Photography: Charlotte Tolhurst for new recipe photography, and Jodi Moreno for the recipe photography on pages 32–33, 36–37, 62–63, 76–77, 118–119, 122–123, 126–127, 170–171, 180–181, 185, 192, 200–201, 208–209, 212–213, 230, and 239.
Photography art direction: Sara Robin, Geoff Fennell.
Food styling: Kate Wesson.
Prop styling: Rob Merrett.
Additonal image retouching: Adam Brackenberry, Tom Morse.
Technical support: Sonia Charbonnier.
Recipe testing: Laura Camerer Cuss, Katy Greenwood, and Jill Weatherburn.
Additional editorial work: Jill Weatherburn.
Proofreading: Katie Golsby, Dorothy Kikon, Janashree Singha, and Manasvi Vohra.
Indexing: Vanessa Bird.

All photography and artworks
© Dorling Kindersley